THE RADIO TALK

THE RADIO TALK

A PRACTICAL STUDY OF THE ART AND CRAFT OF TALKS BROADCASTING

by

JANET DUNBAR

author of
"The Early Victorian Woman"

GEORGE G. HARRAP & CO. LTD
LONDON   TORONTO   WELLINGTON   SYDNEY

TO

MISS FLORENCE MILNES M.B.E.

with respectful affection

First published in Great Britain 1954
by GEORGE G. HARRAP & CO. LTD
182 High Holborn, London, W.C.1

*Composed in Bembo type and printed by
Western Printing Services Ltd, Bristol
Made in Great Britain*

PREFACE

MOST people who broadcast a talk are not professional broadcasters, public speakers, or other kinds of orators. They are either specialists in their own subjects, or ordinary members of the public with something particular to say. They may have been invited to do one or more talks because of their particular knowledge or experience; or they may have sent in a script which reveals an unusual point of view on a subject, or a striking personality.

A study of the BBC's *Radio Times* over a period brings out the fact—a surprising fact, perhaps—that most people who give talks are amateur broadcasters, in the sense that they are laymen doing what is really a highly specialized job. In this they differ entirely from other broadcasters, like actors and musicians, who must reach a certain standard of technical excellence in their respective professions before they are given radio engagements.

It is, paradoxically enough, the best 'amateur' speaker who makes the best broadcaster, for he will convey the feeling of being natural, which is so refreshing to listen to. The professional broadcaster, with his experience of regular announcing or commentating, is liable to sound too practised, too competent, in a talk. He has been trained to do a certain kind of broadcasting—announcing or commentating—in a professional way: in an impersonal and objective manner for announcing, in a lively reporting style for commentating. The point about a good talk is that it is neither detached nor a piece of straightforward reporting; the individuality of the speaker must come through.

Producers are often asked what kind of talks are "wanted." There is no useful reply to this kind of question. A study of the published programmes over a three-months' period will show that talks are given on every kind of subject: therefore every kind of script is likely to be considered.

¶

It will be noted that I have said nothing about television talks. I believe there is very little scope for straight talks on television. Prominent people are asked, from time to time, to give talks on television—statesmen, politicians, visiting notabilities, and others in the current news. They are there for their personality value, and usually have something of immediate and topical interest to say.

I do not think there is much room, at present, for general talks where the speaker just sits there talking. Television is a visual medium, and it is important to have something to show or do.

There is, of course, room for the illustrated talk; but the emphasis is on the illustrations. For instance, if you came back from Mexico having discovered some new treasures of the Aztecs you would have material for a wonderful talk telling of your adventures. But you would have to show the treasures.

I think that the straight talk is essentially, and only, suitable for sound radio; and I believe that the scope for the future is limitless. Since, then, anybody with something interesting to say may contemplate submitting the script of a talk, this book on one person's ideas on the subject may be of some help.

¶

The quotations from scripts which illustrate various points I want to make throughout the book have all been taken from talks broadcast by the British Broadcasting Corporation. This is because most of my radio work has been done for the BBC, and I naturally have drawn on my own experience and observation of British broadcasting. The discussions I have had with producers and regular broadcasters over a long period have also been mainly concerned with broadcasting in Britain and the BBC's services overseas.

But I have also had argumentative and stimulating conversations with producers and broadcasters from other countries: American, Canadian, South African, Australian, New Zealand, Brazilian, Turkish, French, Indian, Belgian, Spanish, Norwegian, Danish, Bolivian. On studying my notes made after some of these discussions, I find that one thing stands out quite clearly. The principles of a good broadcast talk are valid for every country, every language. I have tried to keep this fact in mind all through the book.

It is difficult, after many years in broadcasting, not to have collected a number of prejudices and perhaps obstinate opinions about talks and talkers. I have also tried to keep this in mind. But a few bees may have escaped from my bonnet now and again. . . .

J.D.

ACKNOWLEDGMENTS

My first thanks are due to the British Broadcasting Corporation for the facilities I have been given to do the research necessary for this book. At the same time I must make it quite clear that no opinion which I have expressed is other than my own, except in the instances where the source has been given.

I am especially grateful to Mrs Dorothy May for her patient and unfailing help over many months.

For permission to quote from their scripts I wish to thank Miss Joyce Castagnoli, Mr Julian Duguid, Sir Arthur Grimble, Mr Bernard Newman, Field-Marshal Sir William Slim, Mr Owen Tweedy, and Miss Veronica Wedgwood; and Mrs James Stephens for permission to quote from one of the late James Stephens's scripts.

CONTENTS

Part 1: Planning the Talk

Part 2: The Script

Part 3: Speaking the Talk

Part I

PLANNING THE TALK

I

THE FACTUAL TALK

My first lesson in the essentials—I might say *the* essential —of a script followed directly on the first talk I ever gave, in 1925. It was a travel talk in which I described a walking-tour round the Devon and Cornish coasts. My father-in-law wrote a charming letter to me about the talk, and added, "But you really must not say that Dunster is in Devon, my dear." He was a Somerset man.

Nowadays a few minutes after the close of a talk in which such a slip had been made there would be indignant telephone calls, and later there would come a few letters from societies of Somerset people (possibly from Devonians too) and a sharp rap from any critic who happened to hear the talk. In the early days of broadcasting listeners were not poised to pounce quite so quickly as they are to-day, and no one else seemed to have noticed the mistake.

My father-in-law's gentle remonstrance was based, not on local patriotism, but on something which he considered to be of fundamental importance: the care one must take not to say anything which might mislead one's hearers. In a talk which gives information, directly or indirectly, that information must be correct, down to the smallest detail. The listener must be able to take accuracy for granted.

13

¶

In preparing a talk for radio it is often the most obvious principle which is ignored. One hesitates to say, for the thousandth time, that the spoken word is different from the written word; yet large numbers of scripts are turned down because the writers have not taken that basic principle into account.

A broadcast talk, *as heard*, "exists sentence by sentence in the thought-stream of the listener; after that it enters the tortuous passages of the fading memory," as Roger Manvell, the critic, says. By the end of a talk the average listener would be hard put to it to give a clear account of the beginning and development of that broadcast. He would probably remember the general drift, and any points which interested him particularly, but little more.

A talk, or an article, printed in a journal is there, and remains there. The reader can re-read any part which he has not been able to understand. It is a whole, a unity.

The listener in no way resembles the reader. He has to be approached in an entirely different way, with due appreciation of the fact that he is expected to assemble pieces of the talk for himself, sentence by sentence, into a coherent whole. It follows that the talk must be logically developed, so that the pieces fit on, one after the other.

If this sounds too machine-made for such an individual thing as a talk think of a good short story which you have heard broadcast. At every pause your instinct is to call out, "And then? So what happened?" You are following the line of the story, connecting up what you heard a moment ago with what you are hearing at the present moment. It is this connecting-up which makes sense, as far as you are concerned.

To go on with the analogy, think next of a stream-of-consciousness story. Here there is very little line, or connecting-thread. It is all atmosphere, overtones and undertones, feelings analysed, and subtle, oblique allusions. Background and characters are stippled in, rather like a painting by Seurat. It can be extraordinarily effective and penetrating—on paper. The eye takes it in, rests for a moment in contemplation, and darts ahead.

What would such a story *sound* like, read on the air? The highly perceptive listener might remember sufficient of the early part to be able to build up some coherent impression: the average listener will make very little of it. For him nothing connects.

The same reactions can be expected from a talk (with the possible exception of those in the Third Programme, where you are talking to a known audience: listeners likely to have the kind of mind trained to fit parentheses and qualifying clauses into their proper places).

For the general listener, an involved talk is a mesh of interlocking phrases which shuts him out. The broadcaster has to remember that all the time. If you want to communicate your ideas you must work them out very carefully, in sequence, so that they are not only easy to grasp at first hearing, but as easy as possible to remember.

Otherwise the listener will switch off—not through boredom, but through frustration. An old gardener friend, who had turned off a talk which I had thought would appeal to him, told me, "I got tired o' listening. 'E did 'op about so."

¶

The majority of talks are factual. That is, they deal with something concrete, something which can be

15

described in terms the listener can immediately recognize.

The general factual talk is perhaps easier to do than any other. When you are describing your job, or a craft, or an adventurous experience, you have something definite to talk about. The problem is not how to assemble your subject-matter—for presumably you have plenty— but what facts to select which are likely to interest the listener, and how to present them in the best way for broadcasting. You are *telling* the listener about your work, or your hobby, or whatever it is: you are not reading him a piece out of a book in a "how-to-do-it" series.

Hugh Ross Williamson, the dramatist, writer, and critic, said, in another context:

> Even the most instructional and accurate feature is really a work of art in that its truthfulness depends on its ability to communicate, and not on its ability to record.

That referred to radio features, but it applies just as aptly to radio talks. It is peculiarly true of a talk that sets out to give concrete facts about solid subjects.

Say you want to tell the listener about your job in an iron-foundry. It is not enough to describe the routine of smelting iron. Somehow, in your narration of fact added to fact, you must also convey to him an awareness of what you see daily: sweat and dirt, flame against darkness, men confidently handling gobbets of red-hot metal.

This ability to *communicate* does not lie in purple writing or picturesque descriptions. It illumines a phrase here, a sentence there. Some people have a gift for interpreting the techniques of their trade. They talk in homely language, laced with sudden, vivid metaphor and simile.

Instead of giving a dull recital of items, they have the power to set the listener's imagination sparking, so that he is filling in all kinds of detail for himself.

There is always a market for talks about people's jobs. We enjoy hearing other people's 'shop'; and series of talks on trades, professions, and crafts come on the air from time to time. The speakers in these series are usually asked because they are known to be good at their particular kind of work, and can also talk intelligibly about it. There is room for other scripts, though; talks from people who have curious occupations, or an unusual point of view about their ordinary jobs.

Listeners are fascinated by people who do out-of-the-ordinary work. A few years ago I edited a series dealing with women in unusual trades. The producer and I had planned the general lines of the series, and I had begun to track down a few possible speakers; but several good scripts turned up unexpectedly from strangers who had heard of the series and had decided to "have a go." We finished up with a list which included a woman builder, a chimney-sweep, a labour-officer in charge of entirely male factory-hands, and a woman who drew the white traffic-lines on the roads.

¶

Among the scripts sent in by the public every week are many travel talks. After an enjoyable holiday a strong impulse comes over some people: they must give a talk on the radio about it.

As a matter of fact, you say, *you* have written a talk of this kind yourself. You have had a delightful holiday in France, and would like to tell others about it.

Thousands of people take holidays in France every

year. They see much the same kind of scenery, and meet the same kind of people. Every summer dozens of scripts describing holidays are submitted. They are often competently written, and describe the marvellous food enthusiastically.

Why are they not broadcast? The answer is that it needs something more than competence to catch a producer's eye. It is this "something more" which cannot be taught or explained. It might be a freshness of approach to an ordinary experience—an instinct for observing the commonplace from a new angle. It might be a feeling for the odd character, a curiosity about the little street curling away from the beaten track. Something out of the ordinary there must be, for the listener is not interested in the holiday-snapshot brand of tourist-travel talk.

¶

The kind of travel talk which does catch and hold the listener's attention is the one which describes everyday life in a far-off country. This is a factual talk given subjectively; a great deal of first-hand information woven into a personal narrative.

The best examples of this type of talk that I ever heard were in a series of talks given by Sir Arthur Grimble on his life in the Gilbert Islands. He did not set out to describe either the scenery or the people. He told of his own experiences, living among them. But at the end of every talk you had the clearest picture of what the people and the places were actually like. You had a knowledge of their customs and traditions, and an extraordinary sense of having actually *been* to the Gilbert Islands.

This was not only due to the speaker's pleasant voice and easy manner—though this made listening a pleasure

—but also because the scripts had been carefully planned and excellently written. Every word, every sentence, was exactly right for its purpose. Strong, supple prose, ideal for the spoken word.

It was also ideal for the written word, as one saw when the talks were later printed in *The Listener*.[1] One was able to analyse the way the theme, incidents illustrating the theme, and personal experience had been dovetailed into a pattern which had been so easy to follow on the air.

Here is an extract from the original script of one of the early talks, which described how the speaker and his wife arrived at the Gilberts after a two months' voyage from England:

> *We had shot the roaring surf into the boat-harbour, and climbed the steep hillside to the Residency, to report present for duty. On our way up, we had passed by the busy work-shops and crushing-mills of the Pacific Phosphate Company, teeming with strenuous workers, white and brown. Half a mile from there, we were in the happy languor of a Micronesian village overleaned by palms, with its flaming poincianas, and chattering children, and smiling bronze men home from fishing who lay about crowned with wreaths of white flowers. Higher still, three hundred feet above the sea, we came to the cricket-field on the island's crest, and stood gasping at its view over the tremendous emptiness of the Pacific.*

Note how skilfully the background is brushed in right at the beginning of the talk: the scene is set in the listener's mind. The speaker goes on to tell of his chief, the Resident Commissioner, who suggests that the young new

[1] And also in the book which Sir Arthur Grimble later published under the title of *A Pattern of Islands* (Murray).

official should begin to learn the native language, and
native manners as well.

*His plan was for me to take lessons first of all from the old
headman of the lovely village of Tabiang below the
Residency. . . . I went to Tabiang village on a day arranged, an hour or so before sunset.*

*A little golden girl of seven, naked save for a wreath of
flowers on her glossy head, ushered me into the headman's
house and spread a fine guest-mat for me to sit upon. Seated
cross-legged on another mat, she explained with gravity that
her grandfather had charged her to entertain me, should I
arrive before his return from fishing. He would not be very
long now, she said; would I like to drink a coconut while
she went on entertaining? When I said yes, please, she
brought in a nut which she had opened very neatly with a
cutlass-knife almost as long as herself, and offered it to me
cupped in both hands, at arms' length, with her head a little
bowed. "You shall be blessed," she murmured as I took it.*

*I did say "Thank you" in reply, but even that was
wrong; I should have returned her blessing, word for word;
and, after that, I should have returned the nut also, for her
to take the first sip of courtesy: and at last, when I had
received it back, I should have said, "Blessings and peace,"
before beginning to drink the milk. All I did—woe is me!—
was to take it, swig it off, and hand it back empty with
another careless "Thank you."*

*She did not run off with it as I expected, but stood
instead, with both arms clasping the nut to her little chest,
examining me over the top of it. "Alas," she said in a
shocked whisper. "Alas! Is that the manners of a young
white chief?"*

*She told me one by one of the sins I have confessed, and
I hung my head in shame, but that was not yet the full tale.*

20

*My final discourtesy had been the crudest of all. In handing
back the empty nut, I had omitted to belch aloud. "How
could I know, when you did not belch," she said, "how
could I know that my food was sweet to you? See, this is
how you should have done it!" She sat, and, handing the
nut back to me with both hands, her earnest eyes fixed on
mine, gave vent to a belch so resonant, it seemed to shake
her elfin form from stem to stern. "That," she said, "is
our idea of good manners."*

*But, luckily, it struck me to beg her to give me another
chance when grandfather came in, and the idea appealed to
her. On the old man's arrival, she sat him on his mat,
smiled at me, and danced out to fetch a nut for each of us.
I made no mistakes this time. The volume of my final
effort surprised and shocked me, but it pleased grandfather
enormously, and the little girl clapped her hands for happiness of heart.*

There are other talks which are factual in another
sense; broadcasts which do not set out to describe places
or people or jobs, but events, often of topical interest.
These might interpret a new Education Act, or give the
practical aspect of other fresh legislation, or fill in the
background to an important item of news.

Most talks of this kind are given by people who have
expert knowledge on the subject. Though many of them
prove to be excellent interpreters and guides, some incline
to overestimate the listener's basic information, and talk
above his head all the way through. Others are obviously
conscious of superior knowledge, and talk like Superior
Persons. A listener who discussed this last type with me
was probably typical of many when he said, "I get irri-
tated by the 'I know-something-you-don't-know' tribe.
I *know* they do, but what are they on the air for? *To tell*

me. You never get that smug manner from the really top people."

You never get smug subject-matter from the top people, either—the kind of text which implies that you must have the same basic information as the speaker has, or what a fool you are.

One of our leading contemporary historians, C. V. Wedgwood, never makes that mistake in her talks. She speaks with the authority of knowledge, but she takes into account the fact that she is a specialist, and the listener is not. Without departing in the slightest degree from her own high standard of scholarship, she is able to interpret her subject for the listener in such a way that he is able to follow her by the light of his own intelligence.

In a series with the general title of "Personality in History," broadcast in the Home Service in 1952, Miss Wedgwood made the 'ordinary' listener concentrate on a subject which he would probably have skimmed over if he had come across it in print. Here are several extracts from the fourth talk in the series, a talk which she called "The Place of Personality":

> *History—so far as it is concerned with personality—appears to be the most uncertain of studies: not a storehouse of truth, but a repository of errors and misunderstandings. Far from being an exact science, it is a body of opinions, rumours, and hearsay, pitted by forgetfulness and bloated by invention.*
>
> *But—let us keep our sense of proportion. Dealing as it does with the experience of human beings in action, could it be reasonably hoped that history would be any more scientific or intelligible than the material with which it is concerned? The human brain is the best instrument of the kind which we know—but it's not a perfect instrument. . . .*

So history, which deals with human beings in the first place—and depends entirely on them for its transmission—could hardly be expected to provide material for scientific conclusions. Yet that is just what human beings . . . seem to expect of it. In fact, history can only be interpreted so as to yield general laws . . . if the human element is largely eliminated. Over immensely long epochs it is occasionally possible to detect what appear to be recurrences and repetitions of the pattern—from which you can deduce a law—but these can only be seen if the human lives which originally formed the living substance of history are so very far away that they resemble nothing more human than the lines of a graph.

Those are the opening sentences of the talk, which goes on to develop ideas concerning the nature and function of history. The argument is sometimes complex, but it is never obscure, and it leaves something for the listener to think hard about.

2

THE SPECIALIZED TALK

Talks for Women

SOME people argue that special programmes for women imply a kind of grown-up children's hour. This is nonsense. It is true that a few speakers in women's programmes adopt a bedside manner which they would not dare put on for a general audience, but that brand of whimsicality can be dealt with by a good producer. It is no argument against having specialized programmes of the kind.

I am sometimes asked—usually by indignant feminists —why there should be programmes for women at all; why not simply treat them as part of the population as far as listening is concerned? The answer is that they are so treated. Audience Research results show that as many women as men listen to the general programmes —usually far more. A special programme is just a recognition that women also have particular interests—just as men have particular interests in, say, sport.

There are many subjects which appeal mainly to women only, subjects which would make boring or unsuitable programmes for family listening at peak hours. Women do most of the shopping, and are, therefore, interested in knowing about quality and prices of consumer goods. They have the care of children, and want to know of ideas and developments in child care. They do the cooking, and like to hear about food values and the cooking of food. Modern home planning and techniques have given them more leisure, and they ask for talks on handicrafts and recreations.

There is sometimes criticism that air-time is given to subjects like beauty, fashion, and household hints, which are written about at length and in detail every week in the women's papers. I was critical of this policy myself for a long time; it seemed to me that radio talks for women should only tell them about things, people, and places they were not likely to learn about from other sources.

I came to change my opinion when I found that the average woman listener liked to have practical talks of this kind, whether she read articles about them in magazines or not. Discussions at meetings of women's organizations brought this out again and again. I well remember one listener defending radio household hints on the ground that she never forgot those she heard on the air, while she never remembered those she read in the paper. Another woman made the point that the absence of advertising gave her more confidence in household and housekeeping talks; she felt that they were not 'inspired.' She had lived in America, where, she said, she had accustomed herself to questioning radio recommendations of anything connected with the household.

Talks on domestic matters, however, form a very small part of the regular programmes for women. It would be difficult to find programmes with more variety. Lord Simon of Wythenshawe, in a recent book,[1] said that "Woman's Hour" was "a daily hour of real educational value to the housewife." And Mrs Mary Stocks, a mem-

[1] *The BBC from Within* (Gollancz, 1953).

ber of the Beveridge Committee on Broadcasting, said that she considered this same programme to be the most effective piece of mass education in the whole of the BBC output.

I think this is an exaggerated claim, but I am sure that the programme has, by and large, a great deal of influence in taking the average housewife's mind away from her domestic duties, and kindling or reviving her interest in the world outside her home.

As ninety per cent. of the output of programmes for women consists of talks or discussions, there is obviously great scope for scripts on all kinds of subjects—provided that they are thought out on an adult level. That is the really important basis for any talk in this programme, and the only one which will scotch the deprecating "Oh, it's only a woman's talk" attitude. I have heard difficult themes, like intimate personal relationships, and childbirth, treated with truth, tact, and delicacy in these programmes. I have also heard talks on minor themes larded with coy digs at the little woman presumably sitting knitting by the loud-speaker.

It is this latter type of talk which is one blight on a programme for women. An acquaintance of mine once mentioned during a conversation that he had had a very unusual holiday, and had written a script about it; could I suggest a possible market? I mentioned a weekly programme then running, "Mainly for Women." He said, "Oh, then I'll have to write it up differently." "Why?" I asked. He found it difficult to explain. I pressed him, and he admitted that he thought of women listeners as a race apart—unable to read a map, unlikely to understand his descriptions.

At the other end of the scale is the woman who cannot see why these programmes should not be used to push feminist propaganda. Different points of view relating to social and political questions affecting women are, in fact, broadcast from time to time in the women's programmes as well as in general programmes. But it is surely important, in public-service broadcasting, that no one can point to the women's programmes and accuse them of pushing *any* kind of propaganda. What they do —rightly—is to give air-time to speakers who may have strong views on questions affecting women in the community, but who also have enough knowledge, experience, and honesty to be able to put a reasoned case before the uninformed listener.

Talks for Children

There are few people who can plan, write, and broadcast a really good talk for children. But when they are good they are really good.

Among the best talkers I have heard in children's programmes are Helen Henschel, W. R. Dalyell, Stephen King-Hall, Bernard Newman, and Owen Tweedy. Helen Henschel usually talks about music, and she has the gift of making even quite young children understand what music is about. Mr Dalyell talks about art, but he does not spell it with a capital A. He knows that nearly all children like to draw, and, without attempting to turn them into artists, he puts it into their minds that the best way to get a lot of fun out of drawing is to use their eyes properly.

Stephen King-Hall often talks about current affairs. He knows that all kinds of children look at newspapers, and he manages, in his own way, to give them some idea of what is going on in the world, in words and images which they can understand.

Bernard Newman is an experienced broadcaster who generally has a very exciting script to begin with, and he can put it over. Owen Tweedy tells of fantastic adventures in the East, talks which are all the more effective because of their quiet delivery.

All these speakers are particularly successful because they have an instinct which enables them to establish contact with their listeners immediately. There is an impression of ease, of complete understanding between speaker and listener, which is as delightful as it is rare.

In studying these speakers, and trying to find out what they have in common that makes them such good broadcasters, two things stand out. They all possess in abundance that indefinable, individual quality which we call personality. That is something inherent in themselves. But there is something else. If you listen to their talks critically you will find that they have taken the greatest care in thinking out their scripts. They have taken the trouble to try to understand the young listener's mind—and they have enough common-sense to realize that they are talking to children in all kinds of homes, uncultured as well as cultured. They therefore develop their themes from the ground upwards.

They are, to begin with, logical: they know that children are naturally logical and take things literally. The theme of the talk is clearly stated or indicated at the beginning, and the young listener is able to settle down to *listen*, knowing unconsciously that he will be able to follow without strain what this grown-up is saying.

What are the principles on which successful broadcasting to children is built? The first thing to grasp is that to children there is no mystery or magic whatever about radio. They take it as a normal part of life, and do not rush home from school, as did an earlier generation, to listen to an Uncle or Aunt on the air. They are, too, more critical of their own programmes than were the children of the Twenties and Thirties. The world of nannies and snug nurseries, implicit in so many programmes for children in the early years, is an unknown world to the modern child. If you choose this kind of background for a talk there is a risk that your young listener will not know what you are talking about.

Now that television is expanding it is more than ever important that you should choose subject-matter very carefully. I do not think that there will be as many viewers as there are listeners for a considerable period, on the score of cost alone. (I am taking it for granted that sound broadcasting will have children's programmes for the foreseeable future.) Still, more and more television-sets are sold every week, and a large number of children have a choice of vision or sound. It is only natural that they should choose vision if there is actually something they want to see. The radio talk must accordingly attract their attention by its subject-matter, and keep their attention by its presentation, if it is going to compete successfully with vision.

Some people declare that the popularity of children's programmes on television will stop them listening altogether to the programmes on sound directed to them. I do not think this will happen where talks are concerned —keeping in mind the proviso I have made in the preceding paragraph.

An experiment was recently made by some teachers I know with a dozen children in the 9–12 age-group. Among other questions relating to broadcasting and television, the children were asked whether they preferred to hear an 'ordinary' talk on sound radio, or to watch the speaker on television.

The answers varied from, "I like to see what he looks like, but I don't want to go on seeing him talking unless he does something," to, "No, I don't want to watch him *saying* things." What emerged was that the children, without exception, preferred listening to 'seeing' a straight talk.

They will not listen, though, unless you can hold them from the beginning. A well-known writer of children's books once told me how she set to work:

"I try to block in my colours very clearly right at the start, so that the child can have something for its imagination to fasten on to straight away."

This referred to writing books for children, but the principle applies even more forcibly in planning talks for young listeners.

An exciting beginning to a talk is a certain way of catching a young listener's attention. Here is how Bernard Newman begins four talks in a series which he gave in 1949, called "Real Life Spies."

(a) *Did you know that spies have to go to school? I am afraid that I have broken many a boy's dream that way. Dozens of them ask me how to become a spy—it sounds so adventurous and glamorous. But when I tell them that they have to go to school—well, that does take a bit of the glamour out of the business, doesn't it? Immediately after the First World War I went to a German spy school in Antwerp, and more recently to one in Germany. They were very interesting indeed . . .*

(b) *Do you know how many spies get caught? Not when they are actually doing their spying, but when they are getting their information home. I remember a spy who was never caught . . .*

(c) *Now, how does the real spy set to work? You know how he does it on the pictures, of course. The glamorous blonde distracts attention while the spy burgles the War Office safe to steal the plans. You don't think that it's quite as easy as that? No, and you're quite right.*

(d) The girls aren't going to like this, but I must say it at once: generally speaking, women make rotten spies.

Having caught his listener's attention, Mr Newman doesn't let him down—another essential in talks for children. An ear-catching beginning which tails off into dull narrative will make the young listener feel that this is a "swizz." Mr Newman has plenty to say, but he does not make the mistake of over-packing his script with one exciting incident after another. He chooses several examples of spies' methods, and works them up into conversations. Here is an example from the script "How the Spy gets his Messages Home." He is describing a talk which he and a French officer had with a spy who had never got caught:

This man used to wander about; he crossed frontiers, passing guards, and censors, and they never caught him out. "Look here," we said, "how did you get away with it all the time?"

"I'll show you. Like to go out?"

We went out, and came back.

"Now, I have a message concealed on me—search me!"

We searched him—and we were fairly good at searching. I remember that I annoyed him by ripping out the linings to his clothes, for a start. But it was no good—we couldn't find a thing.

Then he showed us. His method was very simple— these things usually are when you know. He wrote his message on a little piece of cigarette-paper, crumpled it up into a tiny ball, fished out his glass eye, put the message inside the eye, and then put the glass eye back.

Well, I mean to say, suppose you were a frontier guard —would you have thought of stopping everybody and making them take their eyes out for examination?

It is not everyone who has a ready-made winner like espionage for a subject. But the way in which Mr Newman selects and shapes his material shows that he could hold his young listener on any subject.

What do children like to hear about? I think that they are interested to hear about people and animals. They do not like to listen to descriptions of *things*, unless these are closely connected with the people or animals. They like, too, talks about exciting personal adventures, about hobbies, and about anything relating to science which has a practical application.

The way a talk is put over is closely connected with the subject-matter. I am discussing the problems of actually writing a script in a later chapter, but subject-matter and the words and phrases in which the subject is presented are so closely linked in a talk for children that I am following on with this important point now.

In a talk to an adult audience a poor or pompous speaker may keep his listener's attention if his subject-matter is of outstanding interest. In a talk to children the wrong choice of words or phrasing can ruin the otherwise admirable content of a script.

Children dislike long descriptions of scenery and passages of narrative which have no action or dialogue to break them up. And literary phrases in a talk are meaningless. "He was seized with a fit of silent rage" conveys nothing to them, but, "He was furiously angry, so angry that he couldn't speak," blocks in a situation at once. I recently heard a speaker use the phrase, "The clear texture of the air," when "The air was so clear, you could see the rocks a mile off" would have conveyed his meaning in a flash. "The cocoa-coloured population" is a vague concept to a child. Turn it into "The people we saw on the island were brown—as brown as cocoa," and the child is there.

Simple words, clarity of expression, and sentences that are not over-long: ideally, these are what one aims for. Simple words need not be dull. It is a question of using exactly the right words.

Owen Tweedy's travel talks are full of simple words which are, at the same time, richly evocative. He paints pictures in words. Here are extracts from a talk which he gave, describing a visit to the Damascus Bazaars.

The Damascus Bazaars are as old as time. And they look it. Each one occupies its own special street . . . but wheeled traffic is forbidden. So when, last winter, I went to visit them—and, of course, to shop—my queer, old two-horse cab with its still queerer, unshaven, and baggy-trousered cabby set me down at the Bazaar entrance. And once inside, I was back in the days of long ago. . . .

Bedouin from the desert strode by with their heavy brown cloaks ballooned out behind them, and their womenfolk pattering in their wake . . . and, hanging on to their skirts, troops of barefoot children with coloured beads plaited into their hair. Then an occasional Arab notable on horseback, with a dagger stuck jauntily into his red belt, and the harness of his horse gay with tiny brass bells, and red fringes and tassels. . . .

At the end of the "Street that is Called Straight" stands the Ommayyad Mosque, which, fourteen hundred years ago, used to be a Christian church. . . . Beyond it I was, at last, deep in the real old Damascus. The streets were now mere slits—not wider, or straighter, than ordinary

C   33

lanes. On either side of them, tall, balconied houses nodded crazily at each other. . . .

Beyond the brass and copper Bazaar lay the spice Bazaar. . . . Cloves from Zanzibar, nutmegs from Java, pepper from the Spice Islands, cinnamon from the Moluccas . . . my poor nose was completely bewildered. And so, at last to the scent Bazaar. It just breathed scent at me, as at home here perhaps a room full of newly cut flowers may have sometimes breathed its scent at you. It was just perfection. And the atmosphere of the Bazaar was perfect too. . . . The shopkeepers offered their treasures without fuss and with great dignity. I fell for an old gentleman in a spotless white cloak, with a vast red and yellow turban shading his kindly old eyes. . . . The walls held tier above tier of shelves, all laden with glistening glass-stoppered bottles. . . . The next half-hour was for me complete bliss. For I was taught the drill of scent-buying in Damascus. First he took the stopper out of the bottle. Attached to it was a long tapering glass rod; and when he withdrew it one single drop of the scent remained hanging like dew at the point of the rod. Then I put out my hand, and on my wrist he dropped his dew and smeared it gently on my skin with his forefinger. Then he invited me to smell —violet, attar of roses, orange-flower, lily, and tuber rose. . . .

After I had made my choice and we had agreed prices he embarked on the packing of my purchases. He chose tiny bottles—about the size of my little finger, but each with a stopper and glass rod attached to it. Then, with great care, he filled each in turn, and stood them like a row of soldiers on the counter. Next, he produced round metal containers which looked just like cartridges and were about the same size; and into them disappeared bottle after bottle, each with a wad of cotton-wool to keep it safe. Then tops were

34

screwed on. . . . And the whole of my purchases got safely home with me to London three months later.

And there was a sequel. I sent two cartridges—violet and lily—to my niece in Wales. Unfortunately, the parcel was opened by her daughter, aged five, who proceeded to empty the whole contents over her head. For the next week she was furiously pursued by every bee in the countryside.

Mr Tweedy first blocks in the scene: it has an Arabian Nights quality which makes it glow in the child's mind. Even if the young listener cannot conjure up all the images, which follow each other perhaps a little too quickly at times, there is enough in the brilliant flow of words to keep him listening.

But it is the end of the talk which shows this speaker's instinctive grasp of the young mind. Baghdad and its strangeness and far-away-ness are suddenly brought into focus by someone here at home: a little girl. A naughty little girl who pours scent over herself and is consequently pursued by bees. The strange and the far-away are suddenly side by side with the known and the familiar.

Here is script-writing at its best. This speaker shares with other first-class broadcasters that attribute of genius —an infinite capacity for taking pains—together with a fastidious care in choosing just those words most likely to set a young listener's imagination alight.

Talks for Youth Programmes

Youth programmes offer a field for specialized talks; a wide field, for there are increasing numbers of these programmes. There are consequently opportunities for people with a talent for getting on with "youth." By "youth" one usually means adolescents, a more precise term, if an unattractive one.

Youth programmes have a special appeal for social workers, and consequently a special danger for those sincere, morally earnest people who feel they have a message for the young. Giving radio talks to this age-group—the sixteen- to twenty-year-olds—is the ambition of many people I meet, and it is very difficult to explain to them without badly hurting their feelings that they would be quite hopeless on the air. The didactic impulse—the passion to teach, to inform, to advise—is too often the motive power of their work, and it is didacticism which spoils many scripts intended for youth.

It is no use lecturing adolescents on what they should or should not do. In a youth club when a lecturer begins such a discourse they endure him as long as politeness holds them there. On the radio when the voice coming from the loud-speaker begins exhorting the answer is easy; they simply laugh and switch off.

Yet the right speaker, with the right things to say, can have tremendous influence over the adolescent listener. What is the secret of the right approach? The big-brother attitude? In his attempt to make contact the speaker often tries the hearty approach. This is even worse than moral earnestness. The "Ah, I understand your problems, old man" type of speaker is generally detested, on the air as well as on the platform. Young people in their teens, perplexed by the transition from childhood to the adult world, are usually very sensitive to undertones and overtones in a voice, and to the personality behind the voice. They are quick to resent the slightest touch of phoniness or patronage, and just as quick to appreciate complete sincerity.

I had an example of this not long ago when I asked a group at a youth club their opinion of a speaker we had been listening to in a radio programme. I had met the speaker, and liked him immensely for his integrity and the genuine tolerance and charity of his mind. But I had always felt that his extreme 'university' voice was unfortunate for broadcasting, and I wondered if his enunciation had put off this youth club audience.

Their reply to my question of whether they had liked his talk taught me a good deal about what really mattered in broadcasting. "He's a smasher," they said. "He knows something, he does." Not a word about his voice, or his dry manner.

He had talked to them on a subject of ethical importance, stating in clear but simple terms what it meant to *him*, never once declaring what it should mean to *them*. He was, in fact, sharing an experience with listeners he respected. They sensed this, though they would have been unable to put it into words.

Youth audiences like hard facts, especially those dealing with what is going on in the modern world—in science, in the arts, in sport, recreation, and amusements. And it is no use trying to give them what you think they *ought* to like—at least, not in that spirit. You are more likely to have a script favourably considered for these programmes if it is clear that you are writing something which very much interests *you*. If that comes through with sufficient force there is a strong possibility that it will also interest your audience.

Talks for Schools

In her foreword to Richard Palmer's survey of School Broadcasting,[1] Mary Somerville writes:

[1] *School Broadcasting in Britain*, by Richard Palmer (BBC, 1947).

Three main trends of development from the early days of broadcasting to the present day . . . are the continual exploration of the special properties of radio and their adaptation to provide imaginative experience for children on which their own teachers may profitably build; the application of teaching experience to the selection and presentation of material; and the growth of a close partnership between the BBC and the educational system it seeks to serve.

The scriptwriter who is ambitious to give talks to schools would be wise to study that foreword, as well as the School Broadcasting service as a whole. Mr Palmer's book would be a valuable starting-point for this study, for it is an account of an experiment, of pioneers who made mistakes and learnt from them. What the aspiring speaker will soon realize is that the present service—admitted to be the best in the world—has been built on solid, hard-bought experience.

School Broadcasting is a specialized service, and talks are commissioned or selected on a different basis from that in other departments of the BBC. To begin with, it is not the BBC which controls policy in School Broadcasting; it is the School Broadcasting Council. This widely based body has grown from the Central Council for School Broadcasting, which the BBC initiated in 1929, to advise on the most effective way in which a broadcasting service could best be used as an ancillary to the state educational system.

Teachers, local educational authorities, and the Ministry of Education are all represented on the committees of the School Broadcasting Council. The staff of the School Department at the BBC work in close touch with the Council; it is their job to carry out the Council's policy.

38

These producers have, most of them, been teachers, and are trained in broadcasting technique. They are thus doubly qualified for their special work.

There are also regional Education Officers who act as links between the schools, the Council, and the School Broadcasting Department. These officers listen to programmes in the class-room with the teachers of 'listening' schools, and pass on comments and criticisms. The teacher and the Education Officer are able to note whether the children's attention wanders at any point in a broadcast, or whether they seem worried by words or phrases. It is this first-hand evidence of children's reactions which is so useful to producers commissioning scripts.

With the exception of Current Affairs programmes, broadcasts to schools are planned on a long-term basis—usually a year ahead. They do not attempt to take over the function of the text-book. They are carefully designed to be integrated with formal school education, not to replace it. The Ullswater Report on Broadcasting, 1935, states that broadcasts to schools "are intended to supplement, not to take the place of, the work of teacher and pupil, and to provide a mental stimulus beyond the ordinary resources of the school."

The speaker who wants to give talks to schools on any subject must, therefore, understand the background of School Broadcasting, and accept the fact that he will be working as one of a team: a team which comprises the child, the teacher, the producer, and himself. He will have to fit his script into a broad framework which has already been agreed upon by school-teachers and radio producers, who have learnt—and are still learning—to know their listeners' needs. He may be strongly individual in his work—and, indeed, this is a great asset—but unless he is also co-operative he is unlikely to be successful in School Broadcasting. A script may have to be shaped to fit into a particular series, or to connect with one of the pamphlets which are issued to the schools for use with certain lessons. To sum up, speakers generally work to a brief, though not a rigid one; there is plenty of scope for individuality to come through.

I have heard it said that to 'get into' School Broadcasting you have to be either a teacher or an expert. Knowledgeable about your particular subject you certainly must be, but you are not expected to 'teach' it. Far more valuable than an ability to teach is the gift of being able to tell a story, to share your knowledge with the child in such a way as to stimulate his imagination. This is the key to the child's attention, and to his mind.

In a Survey of School Broadcasting made in Kent in 1927 it was found that the listening children responded more quickly to this kind of broadcast than to any other: ". . . almost any form of story, let it be fiction or narrative of experience, gave them more to build on than the most skilful exposition which lacked this story quality."

The ideal speaker in School Broadcasting would be one who was a specialist in his own subject, knew a fair amount about modern education, and had had sufficient experience in radio to appreciate the possibilities and limitations of the medium—together with an instinct for thinking *with* his listener, in any school age-group.

There are a number of speakers so equipped, as you can hear if you listen regularly to school broadcasts. But one cannot always measure up to the ideal. The man with special knowledge, who is able to apprehend what School Broadcasting is trying to do, will not find the lack of broadcasting technique a drawback if he has the essential qualities for the work.

The Biographical Talk

One summer in the nineteen-twenties, while I was on holiday in the Cévennes, I met on a train a party of English people who were getting off at a small station to make a pilgrimage. They were going to visit R. L. Stevenson's landlady—the one who is mentioned in *Travels with a Donkey*. I was astonished to learn that she was still alive, and at their invitation joined the party when they left the train.

We were directed to a prosperous little shop, where a shrewd, middle-aged woman who sold lace presented to us a very old lady in a white lace cap and 'best' black dress: "*Ma belle-mère*—the landlady of the writer, Monsieur Stevenson."

The party surrounded her, chattering questions. What had Stevenson been like? "*Très honnête*," said the old lady. That was all she could remember of the chance lodger of those far-away days. "*Très honnête*," she told us with a grave smile, while her daughter-in-law sold us lace mats and suggested that other English visitors would surely be interested to visit the landlady of Monsieur Stevenson.

The party were soon busy with tea and cakes, and I went back to talk to the old lady. I know now that what I wanted from her was a portrait in *words*. I wanted her to say, "Yes, I knew him. He looked like this—and he spoke thus—and I remember well how . . ."

I had read much about R.L.S., I had seen many photographs and portraits of him. But here was a living link. If only the old lady could remember! All that I had read seemed oddly far away. I wanted to be *told* about the man.

"*Très honnête*"—that was all she could recollect,

adding, when she saw my disappointment, "*Très gentil.*"
And to this day, when I hear R.L.S. mentioned or open
a book of his the first thought that comes to me is, "*Très
honnête—très gentil.*"

Listening to people linked with men and women of the
immediate past is one of the great pleasures of having
radio. In days to come we shall remember Max Beerbohm talking about Beerbohm Tree, Gilbert Murray
talking about the Oxford notables of his day, Bertrand
Russell recollecting his contemporaries.

It is not only talks about the famous or the notorious
that the listener finds absorbing. Some one quite unknown, obscure, can be so clearly and affectionately
remembered that the speaker succeeds in communicating
a living portrait to you, the unseen listener, who never
knew or heard of the original.

I quote again from one of Sir Arthur Grimble's scripts.
"Portrait Sketch" is an example of this kind of talk.

> *I first met George Murdoch on Abemama Island in* 1917,
> *when I took over from him as District Officer, Central
> Gilberts. . . . He settled down on the near-by island of
> Euria and opened a trading-station there. I never knew an
> official in retirement happier than he was. He had married
> his third wife not long before retiring. . . . The compound
> of his trade-store above the shining beach was always a
> hurly-burly of incredibly active infants as freckled and
> Scottish-looking as himself. He would sit . . . gazing out
> at the wild tangle of them with infinite satisfaction, murmur-
> ing, "Why did I not spend all my life at this . . . just
> gathering copra and making babies? Can ye tell me that,
> now?"*
>
> *He was a little sandy-grey man, as wiry and alert as a
> fox-terrier, always spotlessly turned out in starched ducks.*

There was mastery in his jutting beak of a nose and the deliberate, waxed bristle of his sergeant-major's moustache, but caution and humour, too, shone in the pale blue twinkle of his eyes from under the tufted brows. He never told me his personal story as a continuous tale, but from time to time he would turn aside into odd, stark little scenes out of it. . . .

He was born at Greenock in 1857, the son of a small painter and glazier. . . . At twelve years old he began coughing blood. So, on the doctor's advice that a long voyage might do him good, his parents got him employed as captain's boy in a barque sailing for New Zealand.

The captain was a very fine man except when drunk, which was nearly all the time. . . . The sick child deserted ship at Auckland with a spare shirt and his next most valued possession, a toy monkey on a stick, wrapped up in it. Some one had told him of the blessed climate of the Central Pacific Islands, and he had made up his mind to get there somehow. He spent three months in the strange city looking for his chance. I never heard what he did to keep himself alive; all George would say about it was, "I did not beg, I did not steal, and the monkey was grand company; my mother gave it to me the day I left home." He found a job at last as captain's boy in a barquentine trading up to the Marshall and Gilbert Islands. . . .

The next fragment is the story of how Benjamin Corrie befriended him in the Gilberts. Benjamin was a sternly religious but not teetotal Yorkshireman who ran a successful trade-store. . . . He [George] was allowed at first to idle daylong by the lagoon-side bathing whenever he liked, and fortified by enormous doses of shark-liver oil. In three months he was spitting no more blood, in six his cough was gone. Every evening Ben gave him two hours' teaching. There was no heavy discipline until his lungs were healed

. . . the exquisite copperplate script he learned from Ben was beaten into him "with the buckle end of a leather belt." "The Book of Genesis was my first reading primer," he used to say. "Beginning with that I read every chapter aloud to Ben straight through to the last o' Revelations. I was rising eighteen before we came to the end, and that finished my schooldays. He never thrashed me after that, except when I argued with him about the Scriptures."

This is more than a sketch; it is a portrait in depth. One feels one knows what George Murdoch's life was like from boyhood to old age. It is this power on the part of the speaker to evoke real people which triggers off the listener's mind and enlarges his understanding.

¶

There is an increasing demand in broadcasting for the 'Profile' type of talk: a character-sketch which is the radio equivalent of an obituary appreciation in a responsible journal of someone recently dead.

These broadcast tributes are generally unexceptionable —and dull. They are inevitably one-sided. A man's achievements are built up, brick by brick, mortared by abstract words: "Kind," "Generous," "Hard-working," "Ever ready to put his experience at the disposal of the young."

The wall grows higher, until it hides the man. If only the speaker would knock out a brick or two, even if it means leaving holes in the wall of virtues and achievements! If, instead of the guarded, "Perhaps he was not altogether an easy man to deal with," we got "He was a difficult man. You found that out if you worked for him: he drove you as hard as he drove himself." That tells you something about the real man—and also his kinship with ourselves, conscious of weaknesses and human failings as we are.

It is not easy to give a memorial portrait or profile which shows its subject in a realistic and honest light. It would give pain to his relatives and close friends, and might leave distorted impressions in the listener's mind when it was only intended to balance virtues and failings.

But is it not time that we got away from the parish-magazine type of obituary, away from the clichés, the generalizations, the earnest tributes, which are so high-sounding, and which mean so little to the listener? What he wants is a positive impression of a personality: a sense of special character, of idiosyncrasy. The problem for the speaker is to get that across without festooning his subject with rose-coloured labels.

The Autobiographical Talk

Perhaps the only authentic word-portrait of a man is the one he draws of himself.

Is the autobiographical talk going to be the type of personal talk which is essentially of and for radio, and for no other medium?

In print, the autobiography is there for the record, and it is bound to be selective, weighted with wisdom in this place and that, carefully revealing—rarely self-revealing.

But when a man *talks* about himself the carefulness sometimes slips, and then authentic experience comes through. He may consciously wish to present the best of his life. But in a longish talk other things will dart through now and then: the bitter taste of disappointment; dislikes and detestations. These will be on the record too, but only on a script which remains in a file. So far as the listener is concerned the words have come and gone. The speaker, aware of this, feels an unconscious loosening of inhibitions, and talks far more freely—and maybe more honestly—than he would write about himself.

There might not even be a script. Given the right man —articulate without being verbose—the producer could discuss with him beforehand a few headings to act as a guide, and then leave him to talk.

It sounds a wonderful opportunity for the exhibitionists, the romancers. No doubt there will be plenty of bogus autobiographies sent along in the hope of impressing producers. But the genuine personal story has usually a ring about it which is unmistakable.

I well remember an old farmer telling me about his early boyhood in the Northern fells, and his changing attitude to life as he approached middle-age. His theme was not, as it might so easily have been, old days and ways compared with the hurly-burly of modern life. What he communicated to me—a stranger—was something intensely personal: the struggle he had had in young manhood to accept the fact that the earth he tilled and the stock he fed belonged to a family who "never bided in their great house for more than a month in the year." He had longed since boyhood to have his own farm, and in the end had actually emigrated to earn money enough to save. At the end of twenty years he came back with enough to buy a share in a farm. Now the place was his.

"You ought to write a book about it," I said. He replied that it wouldn't go down into written words; but he could *tell* about it, for in the telling he was going through it all again.

I think I remember that old farmer particularly, because he instinctively gave what would have been a fine broadcast. He did not pile detail on detail, nor were there any reminiscences. No "This is what life has taught me" line, no homely philosophy. It was simply a man talking about what he had done in his past, and why; he was not concerned to impress, but just to tell.

Here is the essence of radio talking—if it can be caught and put on the air.

3

THE PERSONAL TALK

THIS is the kind of talk which most people like best. "I was there . . ." "I saw it . . ."—these are the words with an immediate appeal to the unseen listener. I am taking it for granted that the talk told in the first person and describing an experience—physical, spiritual, or mental—is genuine. No doubt a number of people get away with talks which are highly embroidered envelopes containing a few grains of fact. Producers cannot always check up on the genuineness of a personal talk. I would only suggest that the proper market for this type of script is the short-story department.

The real personal talk appeals to the majority of listeners because it is given subjectively; it has a highly individual flavour. A talk *by* a person is much more interesting than a talk *about* him—an old journalistic cliché, and more applicable to broadcasting than to any other form of communication.

You have only to compare a first-class eyewitness account of a disaster with a short description given by some one who was actually in it. I am thinking of the East Coast floods of early 1953. I heard several excellent, restrained reports about the devastation given on the air. Then in one programme I heard a two-minute account broadcast by a woman who had wakened to find the

48

floodwater in her bedroom. She had a halting delivery and a limited choice of words, but that short, rather monotonous description brought home the horror of the entire disaster in a way that the accomplished reporting had not been able to do.

People sometimes feel impelled to give an intensely personal talk because it might be of help to others. I remember a most poignant talk given by a woman who had lost her child. She described her attempts to get back to a normal way of looking at life again. This talk was not commissioned; it was sent in unsolicited. Listening to it, I found it almost unbearable, because of its very courage and beauty. If it had been in the least bit phoney or sentimental I should have found it unbearable in another sense, and would have switched off at once. True feeling, complete sincerity, is what makes such a talk possible on the air.

A personal talk which caused a great deal of controversy a few years ago was given by a student nurse, who spoke about her first reactions to hospital life. She did not take the conventional attitude towards her job; she had a curiously naïve yet penetrating apprehension of ward life. She would not have written such a talk if she had been five years older, but as a record of a sensitive girl's impressions it had validity.

The angry correspondence which followed this broadcast was an indication of the integrity of the talk, for though so many people disagreed, sometimes quite violently, with the student nurse's opinions, few questioned her sincerity.

Here are several extracts from her script:

A girl is walking down a wide, white corridor. It smells of . . . ether and antiseptic. . . . The girl's mind is dancing.

D

. . . She hears the crisp rustle of a new white apron against a new blue cotton frock. She is terribly conscious of the big scarlet cross she carries upon her breast, and she feels like a crusader wearing it. . . .

In the ward in the big hospital she finds blood. Only it smells sickly and goes along with sweat and muck. And the bright red blood is stemmed, and the fresh new wound becomes old, and there is a stench. The nurse turns pale and her eyes lose focus, and she faints. . . .

The wound is covered and the smell is checked, and everything is so bright and bustling and busy, and the sense of well-being through power and mercy is exhilarating. After the first struggle against nausea is won, and she has told herself twenty times not to quit, the nurse becomes used to it. It is only when she is low and alone, and thinks, that she feels sick.

They call her the Little Nurse, for her smile is sweet and they know nothing of the suppression, of anger, irritation, opinion—the careful control she keeps on herself. And she endows each patient with the sensitive emotions that are hers, and bonds of understanding and sympathy are tied by her, and tie only her. . . .

He lies there, a little boy in a ward of men. He is nineteen, and has been in the Navy for three months. . . . He has tuberculosis, and gets to know about this. He doesn't say anything, but the Little Nurse guesses he knows. . . . He doesn't sleep for more than twelve hours all told during the whole of the following week.

She watches him going down. The transparency of his face reminds her of arum lilies. . . . She wants to cry, or yell or curse. She stirs his medicine for a long time to regain her self-control. When she gives him the glass, she winks at him. He likes this and chuckles. . . .

No. 10 is dead. . . . She doesn't sleep well for two days

because she allows her mind to dwell upon and over-emphasize the sweet qualities of his personality.

Her new patient is smiling. He smiles at the Little Nurse. . . . Then the smiling eyes become clouded with pain, and now the Little Nurse comes into her own. She sympathizes and reassures. She watches and works. She knows his every want. The patient, in his agony, holds hard to his nurse, and the grateful looks and words he gives lift her heart to the skies.

He recovers, and the Little Nurse is transferred to another ward. She visits him. She discovers that his smiles are being received by another nurse. . . . He has forgotten. . . . But her conscience asks her, Do you remember No. 10?

An emergency call comes through; a ship has struck a mine off the coast, and they are bringing in the casualties. . . .

The nurses who are picked are very pleased. . . . Twelve hours later, they return. Their aprons are pretty dirty, for the men were covered with oil. They are all very elated, despite their tiredness, and they talk excitedly throughout their supper. The Little Nurse realizes in awe, We are glad to have juggled with human life all day. It has given us a big emotional kick. She feels sick at herself. . . .

And now the Little Nurse is in the depths of despair. She concludes miserably that there is no glory. . . . She ceases to believe there is a God. . . .

A girl is walking down a wide, white corridor. . . . Outside, the bombs are dropping. And now the Little Nurse is under a pile of debris working upon a body. . . . And whether the body be male or female does not enter into the matter. What matters alone is that the heart continues beating. . . .

The wreckage above is creaking—is falling, and does fall. . . .

With the mending of her body, the mind of the Little Nurse is healed. . . . She reaches this conclusion:

It is about one per cent. glory, this living. It's about ninety per cent. stock emotions, and instincts, and reactions with sex, vanity, and gratifications of conscience. But there is one per cent. real glory, and that is worth fighting for. The giving for its own sake—that is worth fighting for. Yes, it is.

Perhaps one of the most remarkable personal talks I ever heard was by a member of "Alcoholics Anonymous." This is an organization which tries to help people who cannot of their own accord subdue a weakness for drinking too much, and its members remain anonymous. I had never heard of it before; I think its existence was a surprise to most listeners.

The speaker was frank, but he showed none of the self-reproach which would have embarrassed the listener. He described his cravings, and the attempt he was making, with the help of this organization, to regain his self-mastery. Some of the facts which he gave were grim enough, but nowhere were they emotional or sensational. This was a plainly told story of a near-tragedy, related in ordinary language, and informed by restraint and intelligence.

There is a kind of personal talk in which the broadcaster does not talk of himself or his own experiences, but does something far more difficult: he tries to analyse one of the fundamental human qualities. There have been many attempts to illustrate such qualities by anecdotes shot through with homespun philosophy; but few people are able to define what seems to be undefinable.

The classic talk on the highest level in this genre might well be the inspiring broadcast which Field-Marshal Sir William Slim gave in November 1946 in the Home Service. He called it, "What Is Courage?" and in it he put before the listener, with clarity and simplicity, what seemed to him to lie at the heart of this most supreme of all qualities:

I don't believe there's a man who wouldn't in his heart of hearts rather be called brave than have any other virtue attributed to him. And this elemental, if you like unreasoning male attitude is a sound one, because courage is not merely a virtue; it is the virtue. . . .

Courage is a mental state—an affair of the spirit—and so it gets its strength from spiritual and intellectual sources. The way in which these spiritual and intellectual elements are blended, I think, produces roughly two types of courage. The first, an emotional state which urges a man to risk injury or death—physical courage. The second, a more reasoning attitude which enables him coolly to stake career, happiness, his whole future on his judgment of what he thinks either right or worth while—moral courage.

Now these two types of courage, physical and moral, are very distinct. I've known many men who had marked physical courage but lacked moral courage. Some of them were in high places, but they failed to be great in themselves because they lacked it. On the other hand I've seen men who undoubtedly possessed moral courage very cautious about taking physical risks. But I've never met a man with moral courage who wouldn't, when it was really necessary, face bodily danger. Moral courage is a higher and rarer virtue than physical courage. . . .

Courage, you know, is like having money in the bank. We start with a certain capital of courage, some large, some small, and we proceed to draw on our balance, for don't forget, courage is an expendable quality. We can use it up. If there are heavy, and, what is more serious, if there are continuous, calls on our courage we begin to overdraw.

If we go on overdrawing, we go bankrupt—we break down. . . .

There are, of course, some people whose capital is so small that it is not worth while employing them in peace or war in any job requiring courage—they overdraw too quickly. With us these types are surprisingly few. Complete cowards are almost non-existent. Another matter for astonishment is the large number of men and women in any group who will behave in emergency with extreme gallantry. . . . I should say that those who perform individual acts of the highest physical courage are usually drawn from one of two categories. Either those with quick intelligence and vivid imagination, or those without imagination and with minds fixed on the practical business of living. You might almost say, I suppose, those who live on their nerves and those who haven't got any nerves. The one suddenly sees the crisis, his imagination flashes the opportunity, and he acts. The other meets the situation, without finding it so very unusual, and deals with it in a matter-of-fact way. . . .

Now, I suppose because I'm a soldier, I've talked most of courage in men at war, but the fighting man is the last to claim a monopoly in courage. Many a soldier in this last war has steeled himself in battle with the thought of what his civilian fellow-countrymen and women were enduring and how they were enduring it. Whether women are braver than men I don't know, but I have always found them, when really tested, at least equally brave.

In the retreat from Burma in 1942 I was deeply proud of the troops who staggered into India, exhausted, ragged, reduced to a remnant, but carrying their weapons and ready to turn again and face the enemy. Yet the outstanding impression of courage I carried away from that desperate campaign was from the Indian women refugees. Day after day, mile after mile, they plodded on, through dust or mud, their babies in their arms, children clinging to their skirts, harried by ruthless enemies, strafed from the air, shelterless, caught between the lines in every battle, yet patient, uncomplaining, devoted, thinking only of their families—so very brave.

4

THE CONTROVERSIAL TALK

Philosophical Talks

TALKS on philosophical subjects come on two levels. One kind, which often deals with abstract concepts on a high intellectual plane, is given in the BBC's Third Programme, the frankly cultural evening programme which the BBC launched in 1946, and which aims, in the words of Sir Harold Nicolson, at qualitative rather than quantitative values.

It might be useful at this point to set down the present pattern of broadcasting in Britain, as the way in which controversial talks are put over varies decidedly according to the particular service.

The three main services, the Home, the Light, and the Third, are the BBC's national programmes. There are, in addition, six regional programmes which cover England, Scotland, Wales, and Northern Ireland. The following quotations from the Beveridge Committee on Broadcasting give some idea of the aims of the main national programmes.

The Home Service, in all its Regional variants, is a carefully balanced programme, designed to appeal to all classes, paying attention to culture at a level at which the ordinary listener can appreciate it; giving talks that will inform the whole democracy, rather than an already informed section. . . .

Flanking it on the one side is the Light Programme, which is devoted to entertainment in its widest sense. Without departing from the standards of integrity and taste which the BBC has set for itself over the whole range of its output, the first aim of the Light Programme is to act as a great 'catchment area' for those who look to broadcasting purely for relaxation and amusement. . . . Having gained the attention and confidence of this broad base of listeners, it is the aim of the Light Programme to interest them in life and the world around them. . . .

Flanking the Home Service on the other side, the Third Programme is designed in general for the serious listener. It aims to broadcast, without regard to length or difficulty, the masterpieces of music, art, and letters which lend themselves to transmission in sound . . . which, if given in the Home Service, would leave little or no room there for anything else. . . .

It is important to note that, while each of the three programmes has its individual character, there is no firm line of demarcation dividing them. The programmes shade into each other, the differences between them being much more marked in approach and treatment than in range of content. . . . It is an essential part of the aim to encourage listeners to move freely within the framework of the three services. . . .

As the target audience for the Third Programme is the 'serious' listener, it is assumed that subjects can be treated seriously. The speakers are, as a rule, specialist writers or university dons. The latter, used to lecturing to students, are apt to use a lecturing style in their broadcasts, though many of them have by now come to accept the fact that the more intimate manner demanded by the microphone is not inconsistent with sound scholarship. Their talks are often full of qualifications and complex ideas; they are broadly able to assume that their listeners have had the kind of education which enables them to follow closely reasoned arguments. It is trained mind speaking to trained minds.

Not only is an academic approach and treatment accepted on the Third Programme, but there is a great freedom of choice in the subjects themselves. Problems of ethics, of non-belief as well as of orthodox faiths, can be dealt with in talks on this level, because a reasonable attitude towards prejudice can fairly be taken for granted in this particular minority listener.

It cannot so easily be taken for granted in the general listener—the one who normally tunes in to the Home or Light programmes. Talks on philosophy in these services have to be on a more popular plane, and they are extremely difficult to write and to put over. Speakers with the necessarily high qualifications to speak on a profound subject like philosophy cannot always express themselves in simple enough terms for the average listener. They do not underrate his intelligence, but they often overrate his ability to follow abstract concepts.

I believe that there is a large potential audience for talks on philosophy which can be made intelligible to the non-intellectual listener. The medieval disputations which are broadcast from time to time attract more than a Third Programme audience. Talks modelled on their pattern of reiterated statement and conclusion would be admirable. A disputation makes no concessions to easy thinking, but it is so clear and logical that a listener who really wants to sharpen his mind can follow without too much strain. A talk with this inherent simplicity of structure would not be too difficult to understand if concrete metaphors and similes were given to help the listener grasp fundamental ideas.

Religious Talks

Until 1928 all political and religious controversy was forbidden to the BBC by the terms of the Government's directions on broadcasting. In 'religion' this meant that only orthodox Christianity could be broadcast, whether in services, sermons, or talks. After 1928, the Government's ban on controversy was relaxed, but the BBC decided that its practice as far as religious broadcasts were concerned would remain unchanged on three grounds: that sectarian or contentious argument was undesirable in the religious field; that the "vast majority" of listeners preferred the time available for religious broadcasts to be used for Christian broadcasts; and that the BBC must not "provoke or offend large numbers of their Christian audience."

This meant that Christian Scientists, Spiritualists, and freethinkers were not invited to broadcast their beliefs, though descriptive talks about other world religions were not excluded under the policy. Moreover, the Chief Rabbi, as the leader of the only large non-Christian religious community in this country, was invited to give talks on the eve of major Jewish festivals.

In practice, up to 1939, religious talks—apart from sermons—were normally confined to Sunday afternoons. They consisted chiefly of expositions of Christian teaching in relation to daily life. There was a long series called "God and the World through Christian Eyes," accounts of missionary work, talks on Church Music, and book reviews.

War conditions stimulated a demand for greater freedom of discussion, and for a wider range of religious subjects. "Lift Up Your Hearts," a five-minute daily talk, broadcast before the 8 o'clock News in the morning, was introduced in 1939. On weekday evenings there were talks and discussions in which the moral and religious principles which should govern society were considered, notably in a series called "The Anvil," in which Christians tried to answer questions sent in by listeners. But the Governors decided that reconsideration of the policy regarding controversial religious broadcasting should be postponed.

After the War the ban on religious controversy was relaxed to a great extent. The Governors made a statement, in which they said[1]:

It is the view of the BBC that broadcasting has a responsibility to do what it can to meet the needs of the millions of people who are to-day hungering after information on religious issues. The Corporation's highest duty in this, as in other fields, is towards the search for truth. The Governors recognize that this must involve the broadcasting of conflicting views; but they are of the opinion that affirmation of widely differing beliefs and of unbeliefs can be made constructively, and discussions conducted on such a plane that the controversy, which is bound to be an incidental to the primary purpose, shall not wound reasonable people, or transgress the bounds of courtesy and good taste. The BBC will exercise its editorial responsibility to this end. Such a broadening of policy will be gradual

[1] *Radio Times*, March 14, 1947, p. 3.

and experimental. It must move within the climate of public opinion. But the BBC seeks the freest possible expression of serious and responsible thought.

The religious talks broadcast to-day come into two main categories. The first includes all those which are intended to meet in any way the demands of Christian believers for further instruction in their faith, and to help with their devotions. These talks are related to acts of worship in which a certain community of belief is assumed to exist between broadcaster and listener.

The second category of talks includes those undertaken under the new policy, in which no such community of belief is assumed to exist. Here, Christians and non-Christians discuss matters of belief and practice from a neutral platform, and address themselves largely to listeners who do not share their own particular viewpoints. In many of these talks the most thorough-going criticisms of established religion have been broadcast for some years. They are generally produced by the Talks Department, and not by the Religious Broadcasting Department.

But most of the talks about religion, and religious talks themselves, continue to be concerned with the teaching of the Churches "in the main stream of historic Christianity," and are arranged by the Religious Broadcasting Department, which is advised by the Central Religious Advisory Committee. The Department's staff consists mainly of clergymen belonging to different denominations. The Committee is representative of the Church of England, the Church of Scotland, the Roman Catholic Church, and the Free Churches which compose the Free Church Council.

Besides talks which deal with personal religious life and questions of Christian doctrine as represented by the above Churches, there is a wide variety of other talks in this field of broadcasting. There are descriptive talks, reporting some event or movement of special interest to Christian listeners; for instance, this week, as I write, there is a talk by the Secretary of the Church Missionary Society of East Asia, in which he tells of the situation in Hong Kong and its relation to the Chinese hinterland.

Another kind of talk is one in which some subject of doctrine, Church history, or morals is expounded as an introduction to group discussion—such as those in a series of talks on "Reading the Bible," which took the place of sermons in recent Sunday broadcasts.

But the regular programmes which most listeners like best are probably "Lift Up Your Hearts" and "The Silver Lining." In this latter weekly programme there are many different kinds of speakers. Sometimes it is a minister of religion or a doctor or psychologist, helping listeners with their problems. At other times it may be a layman, telling of his own experience of grief or loss in such a way as to give solace and comfort to others. Many of the talks are not explicitly Christian, though Christian values are always assumed.

¶

Who listens to talks on religion? The religious man or woman: people who go to church?

The present Head of Religious Broadcasting writes that

. . . the majority of those who now listen to the main religious broadcasts are not regular church-goers. Evidence collected and tested week by week for years indicates that something like one third of the adult population hears at least one religious broadcast a

Sunday—and . . . at least half of these listeners will not have been to church the same day.

One might argue that people who listen comfortably at home to religious broadcasts consider them as a substitute for church-going. But it is unlikely that people who really want to go to church think that a broadcast can take the place of a service. If church means anything to them they go. It is very probable that—apart from invalids and old people who cannot attend church for physical reasons—a very large number of listeners to religious broadcasts are non-church-goers.

The quotation from the Head of Religious Broadcasting referred particularly to services. The same observation, however, probably applies to religious talks. There is a very large audience, actual and potential, for talks which deal with the fundamentals of faith and belief. Contributions by laymen are particularly popular. Series of talks on "My Faith and My Job," to which individual laymen from different occupations and professions contribute, arouse considerable interest, and it is clear that talks on this broad basis have a special appeal for the non-religious listener.

Here, then, is a field for talks broadcasting which is of great importance. But a speaker who wishes to enter it must be actuated by more than piety and goodwill. Besides the essential quality of sincerity, a speaker needs to be gifted with that special kind of understanding which not only comprehends people who have religious faith, but also those who are seeking something to live by, and have not yet found it.

Political Talks

Talks of a political nature are regularly heard on the air. As H. G. Nicholas says:[1]

> There are few political views of any importance which do not get a hearing. To a remarkable degree the BBC has been successful in applying on the air the principle that the Speaker applies in the House of Commons, of recognizing individuals not in proportion to the numerical strength of their support, but on the basis of the interest of the views they entertain. Minorities, in politics as in other fields, have been well served. . . .

Like other controversial subjects, politics breed fanatical partisans. The most retiring people, those who normally detest publicity, become convinced at some moment that they have a 'call' to tell the nation what they feel about their party—and about the opposing parties too.

This is one of the subjects, however, which is potential dynamite, and suggestions for political talks from unknown members of the public go through a fine sieve.

The present policy is to balance political views and comment, and talks are vetted accordingly. It is not generally realized that talks from Britain—not only in the overseas services but those picked up on the home wave-lengths—are listened to all over the world, and that broadcast political talks are accepted by many foreigners as the official views of the prevailing Government. We, in this country, know that this conception is not true and never has been true, but many foreigners think it *is* true, and no amount of argument makes them think otherwise.

It is not surprising, therefore, that unsolicited scripts on

[1] *BBC Quarterly*, vol. vi (1951).

politics are seldom accepted. It is usual for Members of Parliament, or known experts on world affairs, to be asked to give talks of this kind. Not only do they have special knowledge of home and foreign affairs, but they have been trained to see events in perspective: to assess the importance of topical happenings against the current world situation.

This may sound an abstraction—or, as I heard it expressed by my gardener friend, "blah-blah-blah." It is, in fact, the crux of the problem of broadcasting political talks. The average listener, like my gardener friend, has neither the knowledge to judge, nor the inclination to think out, home politics in relation to world-wide events. If pressed for an opinion, he is likely to echo the newspaper which is his daily tipple.

The speaker asked to give a political talk is a trained commentator, used to reading all the home newspapers, together with many foreign journals. He has travelled abroad a good deal, and has enough experience of foreign habits of thought and expression to be able to interpret statements and speeches, and to extract whatever hard-core information there is in them. It is reasonable to ask a man with such a background to give political talks, as he is more likely to be temperate, balanced, and accurate in what he says than a person with no such experience.

There are some people who become slightly unbalanced at the mention of the word 'balance' in connexion with broadcasting. They maintain that what is needed in the whole field of radio talks is far less balance, far more controversy.

These two words are generally said as if they had entirely opposite meanings. In fact, they complement each other. Without controversy there would be nothing to balance. Controversy means argument, which means the expression of more than one point of view—opposing points of view, if you like, but there are many degrees of opposition. In some controversial issues there are half a dozen points of view, all conflicting.

So far as one can judge from using one's own ears, there has always been plenty of controversy on the air. If, as some people declare, one opinion generally cancels out another, I would submit that this is a good thing; the ground is then clear when something really positive and constructive is said: something which cannot easily be cancelled out.

Listening to many sides of a question is the only possible way—as I see it—of helping the layman to form conclusions for himself. The conclusions may be wrong ones, but at least he has not been persuaded into them by demagogic oratory. Listeners are people, not sheep. And most people like to arrive at decisions themselves.

Besides the democratic principle that public-service broadcasting should provide a forum, and not have political opinions of its own, there is the plain fact that an impartial radio service inspires confidence in its integrity.

"It was of first importance that the service should be trusted," wrote Lord Reith, referring to the early days of broadcasting.

Foreigners who live in countries where political broadcasting is not impartial would be the best judges if it came to comparing different systems.

¶

There is so much misconception on the subject of political broadcasting that it would be useful to examine what the BBC's policy actually is in practice.

The Beveridge Report on Broadcasting (vol. ii, p. 109) prints an agreement made between the BBC and the leaders of the three political parties. Lord Simon of Wythenshawe, who, as Chairman of the Governors from 1947 to 1952, attended joint meetings stemming from the agreement, gives the following information about party political broadcasts.[1]

> Ministers of the Crown . . . use the radio from time to time for ministerial statements which are factual, or explanatory of government policy, or in the nature of appeals to the public to co-operate in national policies.
>
> Each year a limited number of controversial party political broadcasts are allocated to the leading parties in accordance with their polls at the last General Election. . . .
>
> *General Election Broadcasts.* The BBC decides the number (about twenty-four), the three leading parties decide the allocation between themselves, and also decide whether any broadcasts should be given by any other party. This has been decided on the basis of the number of candidates. . . .
>
> In addition to the above major broadcasts, the BBC is free to invite members of either House to take part in controversial broadcasts of a round table character. It is understood that every effort shall be made to treat the parties fairly in this matter.
>
> No discussions or statements may be broadcast on any issue which is within a fortnight of debate in either House.

[1] *The BBC from Within* (Gollancz, 1953).

Part 2

THE SCRIPT

5

HOW MUCH CAN THE LISTENER UNDERSTAND?

MARGERY FRY once wrote in the *BBC Quarterly*:

> Anything which creates common intercourse and common thinking across economic cracks in the structure of society, which makes it possible for men and women of different ways of life to come together and appreciate one another as human beings, is of untold value to the solidarity of the community.

Substitute the word 'educational' for 'economic,' and you have one of the chief problems which the broadcaster of a talk has to face when he is preparing a script, especially if it is concerned with a serious subject which needs breaking down into easily understood terms.

To whom is the broadcaster talking? Who is the listener? How much can he understand?

That is a question which is continually coming up in broadcasting.

It is not only a question of education. Professor Cyril Burt writes[1]:

> As a result of the psychological testing carried out in the Forces plainly reveal, the inborn intelligence of adult men and women shows only a part correspondence

[1] *BBC Quarterly*, vol. iv (1949–50).

with their actual education, and a still looser correspondence with their actual occupation. No doubt the
average member of the professional class must be more
intelligent than the average workman, because the
former must pass a series of stiff examinations before he
can become a doctor, a lawyer, or teacher. Neverthe-
less, there is a vast amount of overlapping. The bright-
est dustman that I have ever tested had an intelligence
well above the dullest of the doctors I have examined
for a (post-graduate) diploma or degree. And, in comparatively lowly vocations, as any lecturer to W.E.A.
or University Extension classes will readily testify,
there are plenty of highly intelligent and intellectually
inquisitive citizens, who are ready for, and capable of,
hard thinking and sound reasoning, provided only the
problems and the evidence are put to them in a way
that appeals to their interest and experience.

But few of us have met Dr Burt's bright dustman; and
highly intelligent and intellectually inquisitive citizens,
capable of hard thinking and sound reasoning, do not
make up the average listener.

We have to be realists, and to accept the fact that, in
general, what the listener understands is conditioned by
the kind of education he has had. In the words of a social
scientist, Professor Madge, "the class stratification of
these islands is a highly complicated matter."

As it is impossible to broadcast talks designed for each
level of this class stratification, one must do one's best to
appeal to large numbers of them at a time.

The first thing to do, it seems to me, is to approach
the tetchy subject of 'class' as honestly as possible. In
spite of the gradual raising of general educational standards, and the influence of widespread democratic ideas,

there is still on occasion a great deal of hostile feeling between the classes. Broadly speaking, it exists mainly between upper and middle class on the one hand, and lower-middle and working class on the other. It is no use arguing that this division does not or should not exist; you know as well as I do that it does exist, and that it is at the root of much conflict in everyday life, as well as in the political jungle.

I am not here concerned with the principles of our hierarchic system of society, or with the demagogues who insistently press for what they call 'equality.' I am concerned with the care one should take in a broadcast not to exacerbate the fierce resentments which are inevitable as a result of class division.

¶

Thus one's mental attitude towards the planning of a talk is important, before any ideas are put on paper. The first thing to remember is that over 80 per cent. of the population were educated at State schools, and had to set about earning a living at the age of fourteen or fifteen. This education, barely adequate as a preparation for life, does not equip a man—unless he is exceptionally studious by nature—with either a wide vocabulary, an extensive knowledge of literature, or much appreciation of the arts.

Of the 20 per cent. left, about 17 per cent. have had a higher education during the school years, and 3 per cent. of the population have been to a university. It is from this 20 per cent. that most broadcast talks come. This is not only because they can express themselves with ease, but because they have the unconscious confidence of people who write and speak correctly without effort. I must immediately add that scores of people with only the usual State education behind them have made, and will go on making, excellent broadcasts. But they are generally exceptional people. By and large, looking at the pattern of broadcasting as a whole, it is the 20 per cent. who broadcast to the 80 per cent.

The 80 per cent. are quite aware of this fact, and are ready—quite understandably—to flare up at the slightest hint of patronage in a speaker's choice of words, or manner, or intonation. People who have had only a limited education are generally sensitive about their deficiencies, even if they are not articulate about them. And many men and women try their best to make up for these deficiencies in adult life. One has only to visit evening schools to see proof of this hunger for knowledge.

Broadcasting, and especially the broadcasting of talks, meets this need on a much vaster scale than evening institutes can do. The average listener has come to understand something of the complex of experience going on outside his own limited life, and he often listens to talks which do not in the least touch on his own concerns.

I once took part in a survey which was designed to find out why members of a large discussion group— composed mainly of artisans—listened regularly to talks which they admitted were outside their normal range. Setting aside two or three who obviously listened for snob reasons, it came out very clearly that the group listened to such talks because they were conscious that here was a way in which they could make some kind of contact with other minds, wider and richer than their own. Even when the subject was beyond their comprehension, they were eager to follow the line of argument, or to pick up such facts as they could understand.

¶

The intelligibility of broadcast talks has been the subject of several inquiries. In 1950 Professor P. E. Vernon, of London University, studied the intelligibility of Forces Educational broadcasts. Two years later W. A. Belson, of the BBC's Audience Research Department, followed on with an inquiry relating to a regular talks programme, "Topic for To-night," continuing the same broad line of research, but taking other factors into account.

These inquiries were concerned with special series of broadcasts, but many of the findings apply to radio talks in general.

Professor Vernon's objectives[1] were to try to measure the extent to which broadcasts primarily intended to convey information are understood by their listeners, and to attempt to assess those qualities in a talk which make it intelligible to the listener. Over 4000 'test' papers were studied, the different educational levels of the people taking part being similar to the ratios which apply to the whole population. The panel of judges for the inquiry included three experienced talks producers as well as several psychologists.

The inquiry was concerned *only* with what the test listeners could understand while actually listening to a broadcast. No attempt was made to find out how much they could remember afterwards. It was the immediate impact of the talk which was being studied.

The methods of obtaining this information were the usual ones followed in social inquiries; the marking was made according to the various educational levels of the

[1] "The Intelligibility of Broadcast Talks," by P. E. Vernon, in *BBC Quarterly*, vol. v (1950).

people taking part. As was to be expected, the higher the mental capacity of the listener, the better he was able immediately to understand the talk being broadcast. Nor was it surprising to find that more than two-thirds of the test-listeners had no great intellectual capacity, as revealed in their answers.

The outstanding fact that emerged from the inquiry as a whole was that listeners' understanding of a broadcast does not depend mainly on their mental capacity to grasp every point, but on the 'interestingness' of the subject. Many of the talks in the test were on current affairs and on science, and contained words and ideas which needed to be listened to with close attention. Yet it was found that they were understood better than other talks which were more simply written, and which used popular devices like dramatization. These last were sometimes described as "boring" and not very intelligible—though they were, in fact, well and clearly written. It was obvious that if the listener found the theme uninteresting, his actual understanding was affected.

The inquiry goes on to list further conclusions which were made by Professor Vernon and his panel.

(a) Broadcasts with less than half a dozen major teaching points are more likely to be intelligible than those with a large number. (A major teaching point is a special point which the speaker wishes to get across. To do this, he expands and stresses it for a minute or two.)

(b) Lucidity and liveliness of style are essential, as opposed to a 'bookish' form of prose. And, in this context, concrete rather than abstract words.

(c) Abstract ideas should have clearly related illustrations, the relevance to the main theme being emphasized —in case the listener pays more attention to the illustrations than to the original point.

(*d*) There should be clear summaries at the end of a factual talk.

There are also a number of obstructive facts which tell against a talk being quickly apprehended by the listener. Talking too fast is one. Literary metaphor is another —"wave of prosperity," "vicious circle." Very long sentences, especially when they have several clauses and parentheses. Speech that attempts to be too conversational, with frequent personal references, repetitions, or incomplete sentences.

There are a number of further points, but the one which emerges most clearly is that a talk which is *interesting* is more easily understood than a talk which is actually easier to follow, but has dull subject-matter. The inquiry indicates that a further line of research might well deal with the question of what constitutes 'interestingness' for the average listener, how interest in a subject can be aroused, and how to make 'dull' subjects interesting.

¶

Mr W. A. Belson's follow-on study in comprehensibility[1] was centred on "Topic for To-night," a five-minute talk given every night from Monday to Friday. This programme is directed to the general listener, and sets out to provide a vignette of background information to some item in the week's news—political, industrial, or economic.

Over a thousand listeners took part in the inquiry, drawn from all sections of the population. They met in groups, but remained anonymous. Each group had a chairman and two people concerned with the administra-

[1] *BBC Quarterly* vol. vii (1952).

tive side of the inquiry. Talks from "Topic for To-night" were played back, and assessments made of each listener's interest in and understanding of what the speaker had said.

Some groups listened under ideal conditions; the atmosphere was easy and informal, there was silence during transmission, and no interruptions.

Ordinary home listening, however, is very different, especially in families. The average radio-set is by no means perfect, and reception is not always good. There are distractions: people talking, the telephone ringing, neighbours dropping in or coming to the door.

Other groups were, therefore, made up of people who said they had listened to the previous night's talk at home. There was no play-back for these listeners, as they had heard the talk already; they took part in the test as a separate group.

The tests for both groups included questions of how much they remembered of the particular talk, and how much they had understood. There were further questions about how much background knowledge they had on the subject. Information about education and occupations was also given. The members of all the groups remained anonymous throughout.

The results of the inquiry tallied closely with what was already known of the general public's understanding of other talks. Short and well-delivered as is "Topic for To-night," the findings show that it tends to be above the heads of most people listening to it. Naturally, some of the groups understood the talks better than others, because of a greater preknowledge of the subject. But, on the whole, the average listener understood only some of the ideas presented, and those not very connectedly.

The talks themselves varied in content, the subjects

ranging from prison reform to divorce, and from the Festival of Britain to Malaya.

The tests showed that some of the talks were less well understood than others, and the scripts were later analysed in various ways.

It was found that the poorly understood talks differed from the others in three respects. First, they took for granted too high a degree of background knowledge in the listener. Second, too many difficult words were used in them. Third, the ideas were not logically developed, to enable the listener to follow the argument easily.

A further criticism was made that no emphasis was put on special points in the talk; this, it was suggested, should have been in the form of a short summing-up at the end.

The conclusions reached in this inquiry help one to understand why many listeners—those whom we call 'average'—find difficulty in following even a short talk of five minutes.

(*a*) The speaker too often takes for granted that the listener knows far more about the subject than he in fact does know.

(*b*) Many of the words used in a talk are unfamiliar and 'bookish.'

(*c*) The onus of piecing a talk together into a coherent whole has been placed on the listener. Instead of having his attention fixed on understanding the various points in the talk as they come along, the listener has to sort out the ideas themselves, so that he is doing a mental jigsaw puzzle when he should be following a clearly stated theme.

6

WHY HAVE A SCRIPT?

THE only person I have ever seen give a straight talk without a script was Eleanor Roosevelt. That was an experience. She sat at the microphone, perfectly at ease, and began. Friendly, informal, full of sound sense, her talk was not only admirable in content but in manner. It had a *shape*. She began on a personal note, introduced a theme, developed that theme, rounded off with a few observations, and came to a natural stop.

Mrs Roosevelt gave that particular talk at short notice, on one of her visits to London. But she had done some hard thinking in the time at her disposal. Even allowing for the fact that she was a practised public speaker and broadcaster in her own country, her performance without a script was a model. The talk had a structure, a framework; each idea followed logically from the preceeding idea. The words she used were simple without being hackneyed. The phrases were varied in length; short when she wanted to get something over crisply, longer when an idea had to be explained.

At the end of the eight minutes which had been put at her disposal she glanced at the clock, and within the next fifty seconds had brought her talk to an end. One could have gone on listening for an hour.

How many people would be able to give an unscripted

talk in such a satisfying fashion? Very few. Quite apart from Mrs Roosevelt's personality, which seems to warm the very air round the loudspeaker, it is her instinctive feeling for form which makes it possible for her to give a first-class talk at short notice, without a script. She seems —as one producer says—to have a clock inside her head.

This is mental discipline of a high order. Such a sense of time betokens unusual clarity of mind and an awareness of the medium of radio.

The trouble with the unscripted broadcaster is the not surprising one of long-windedness. Inexperienced radio speakers lose all sense of time at the microphone, and are often indignant to find that their allotted time is up before they have been able to say half they had intended to say. They *must* have several more minutes, they insist. They seem unaware of the larger pattern of broadcasting in which they are only a small part: they blandly ignore the fact that time is not expandable, and that if they over-run, the programmes which follow will have to be shortened.

Speakers who dislike scripts often argue that excellent speeches are given without notes on platforms. They are indeed—by speakers who have written out, sub-edited, learnt by heart, and rehearsed their speeches beforehand. Once the platform speaker has the secure feeling that he knows exactly what he is going to say, he feels free to be 'spontaneous.' He can choose his pace and vary it, stress some points and pass over others, according to the mood he senses in his audience. He has a barometer of listening faces in front of him to act as a challenge and a stimulus—so that if, by chance, he dries up he has sufficient momentum to pick up the thread of his speech somewhere and improvise until he can get back to the main point.

F   81

The unscripted broadcaster who suddenly goes blank has no sympathetic blur of faces at which he can smile and say, "Now I've forgotten the point I was going to make here. But to turn to another issue . . ." In the studio, the silence can begin to shout as he begins to flounder. The lengthening pauses, the throat-clearings, the repetitions, the desperate attempts to make confusion less confounded by a reiterated, "What I mean is . . ." these are the immediate results of a dry-up, unscripted, in the radio studio.

I have heard producers argue that this need not happen: that an articulate speaker can give a connected talk with only a list of headings jotted down—headings which have been discussed beforehand. I agree; I have heard a few talks of this kind in discussion, and what boiled mutton they have been. A good talk has to be connected, but it has to be so much more, too. Words matter, as well as the thoughts behind them—and how many of us, in everyday speech, are gifted enough to be able to express thoughts in exactly the right words, straight away? Well-chosen words *need* to be chosen; well-chosen sentences take time to frame. In speaking extempore, it is the cliché which rises too quickly to the lips. An intelligent speaker *hears* when he comes out with a hackneyed phrase, and, in an attempt to correct the impression he knows he is making, he may well follow on with generalitics which will land him on the bedrock of banality.

¶

The technique of the edited discussion could probably be adapted to the unscripted talk. Perhaps that will be the compromise accepted by people like myself, who at present are strongly pro-script.

The method with a discussion of this kind is to get speakers round a table, let them argue their heads off, and record it all on tape. A script of the discussion is also prepared. (And very odd reading it usually makes! The things speakers will say off the cuff are incredible, especially when the Chairman is obviously expecting them to speak, and they feel they have to say *something*.) The producer then has an editing session by himself. (If he allowed the speakers to be with him they would clamour to do it all over again—and this would happen every time they re-recorded.)

The producer listens to the playback, following it with the script. He marks passages to be cut out, and proceeds to fashion the rest into some kind of unity, with every point of view given a fair share. The result is often a lively and spontaneous-sounding discussion, with a firm line running through it. The producer is concerned mainly with the argument itself, with the balance of opinions, and with the impact of contrasting personalities.

It does not follow that an *ad lib.* straight talk recorded and edited in the same way would sound equally lively and spontaneous. The producer has not got the same variety of material to work with. He may tell the speaker, "Now, you can say anything you like about your subject —the microphone is yours for twenty minutes or so."

The speaker may say twenty-minutes'-worth—in words. But when the producer comes to listen to the playback, what does he hear? Perhaps four minutes of actual broadcastable material. The rest is taken up with restated points, anecdotes, and far-fetched similes. There is no structure—simply a series of statements, made by the same voice, which the most skilful editing cannot make exciting or interesting.

I am quite aware that the foregoing is a prejudiced

view on my part, and that there are speakers who can be articulate and cogent with no more help than a few headings in front of them. Editing a recording of this kind would mean only cutting out the less interesting of their utterances. A number of people are fluent in this way, especially Members of Parliament and others used to public speaking.

But they are the exceptions. The great majority of talks speakers are, as I said in my Preface, 'amateurs.' After listening to broadcast talks, both inside the studio and at home, for a considerable number of years, I have come to the conclusion that a script is really necessary for most speakers.

The way to get them to deliver the script naturally is to put them in the hands of good producers. A producer who knows his job can make a speaker understand that the script is there as a guide, not as a reading lesson.

7

CHOOSING AND SHAPING THE MATERIAL

TALKS vary in length from about three to fifteen or twenty minutes—except those on the Third Programme, where there is more air-room.

The right length for a talk depends on its subject. If you listen to a number of talks in the current programmes and analyse them immediately afterwards you will find that a good five-minute talk deals with one or two points —not more. These are presented lucidly, unhurriedly, and in the round. A longer talk has naturally more meat in it, but it must be meat which is easily digested. Clarity is the basic essential; if the listener does not know what you are talking about, or has difficulty in following your sequence of ideas, there is no purpose in your broadcasting at all.

Whatever the length of talk you decide on, you should have, to begin with, far more material than you can possibly use. My own method is to get everything I can think of down on to paper in a series of headings. Pages of them—relevant or only slightly related to the main subject: down they go. Some people say they can write a script straight off, without notes. But most regular writers—and trained writers are quick to recognize significant and interesting ideas as they come into the mind —do not rely on a mental selection; they write down masses of facts, ideas, quotations, references, and then they select what they need and shape the talk accordingly.

Amassing facts is not difficult. The art is in choosing and presenting only those which will be interesting to other people. Your impulse is to put in far too many items: to pack the talk to bursting-point with information. It is the didactic impulse—to tell, to teach, to share one's own knowledge. A worthy enough impulse in itself, but it needs the firmest discipline, or else it leads to the kind of broadcast which makes the listener switch off.

The most valuable part of a factual talk is often what you leave out. Your object, in the last analysis, is to give your listener a clear impression of something you know about and he doesn't. To do this effectively you need his co-operation, and you will not get it unless you stimulate his imagination.

A solid talk relentlessly filled with fact upon fact will bludgeon his imagination, not stimulate it. The listener cannot retain in his mind item after item of information; and he is peculiarly allergic to figures, unless they immediately apply to what is being said, or directly concern him.

They must convey something definite. The Chancellor of the Exchequer, used to thinking in millions of pounds, knows that he must translate his Budget proposals on the air. He will say, "Your tobacco is going to cost you more —2d. on a packet of cigarettes—and I hope to raise X-million from this source." This may be depressing and infuriating, but at least you understand what he intends to do to *you*. Or a speaker, in a talk on town-planning, may want to give the listener some idea of population density. He knows that "ninety thousand" has as little meaning to the average person as "seventy-five thousand," in terms of people or square miles. But if he says, "A family in this new town will have a house to itself, and newly married couples will be able to have self-contained flats," he is saying something which the listener can immediately grasp.

If you must give statistics, give the listener a measuring-stick too. And change percentages into 'so many out of every hundred.' The listener knows perfectly well what per cent. means; but the word immediately conjures up forms, and exercise-books with sums, whereas 'so many out of every hundred' belongs to speech.

The question of how many and what kind of facts to choose is difficult to answer when one is asked to interpret something which is, in its very nature, a bulky mass of information.

I had to study these problems some years ago, when I was asked to give a series of talks on the Beveridge Report on Social Insurance, which had just been published. I was to have the woman listener especially in mind.

There was no "Woman's Hour" in those days. The talks were to be given on Sundays, after the One o'clock News, and there would be a fair number of husbands as well as wives listening.

The first thing I had to decide was my approach to the planning of the series. I knew it was little use talking about equity, or the general principles of social insurance. Many people—wage-earners—would already know about the existing State insurance. But Beveridge's scheme took in the whole nation. There would be large numbers of people listening who knew nothing at all about State insurance, or how it worked; they would probably be suspicious of officialdom, too, and would resent the idea of any State 'charity.'

At the same time, practically every listener would want to know, "What is there in it for *me*?"

The only thing to do was to think of the listener as knowing nothing about social insurance; to take it for granted that he had no background knowledge whatever.

I then proceeded to explain how the proposals would affect different people: spinsters, bachelors, married women, mothers, widows, retired people, and so on. I guessed that lists of figures read out on the air would go in at one ear and out of the other; so I broke down contributions and benefits to show how they were related, and tried to use the simplest possible terms throughout. This was not difficult, as the Report itself was a model of clarity and painstaking exposition.

My greatest difficulty was in deciding how to begin each talk so that people who had listened to the News would not switch off as soon as I began. Social insurance sounds a drab subject, and though the Report had been given a great amount of publicity, I was not sure how far the housewife would bother to listen to it being explained yet again.

What I needed was a really strong opening to each talk. It was not for me to dramatize the Report or to 'pep it up' in any way. What I tried to do was to humanize the hard facts. I invented a family, and showed how each member would be affected by the new proposals. It had to be a very large family—but that was part of the convention. All I wanted was that the listener should feel I was talking about human beings—and not about units in a mass.

¶

A producer of my acquaintance, a most cultured and erudite man, once told me that a good talk usually began with an 'ear-fixer.'

I cannot think of a better way of saying that if your talk begins with a striking phrase the listener's attention will at least be caught.

The traveller Julian Duguid is a master of the vivid opening. Here are two examples:

(a) *It seemed a perfectly normal skyscraper, standing on top of a hill. It was twenty-four storeys high, and its white face looked no different from the hundreds of other tall buildings that gleamed in the centre of São Paulo. Yet, in fact, this skyscraper is unique. It is the only one in the world to start to fall down after erection and then to be pushed back into place.*

(b) *Some twenty years ago I used to hunt jaguars on horseback through the forests and swamps of Mato Grosso. It was quite a business to get there. A fortnight by ship to Rio, five days and nights in a train, and then another week in a river-steamer.*

Now, if you were really in a hurry, you could leave London Airport on a Sunday morning, and arrive on Tuesday afternoon.

After that, one *has* to listen. But it is no use beginning a script with an ear-catching phrase and then dropping into dullness. That is the banner-headline trick of journalism. You should so choose and shape your material that it begins on a high note and continues for as long as possible on that level. After a minute or two you can afford to relax the tension.

89

A talk on one continuous note of excitement would be as irritating to listen to as a talk on one note of monotony. Like a high-speed football commentary, it would not give you time to think. The listener to a talk is usually in a relaxed frame of mind, and to keep him at mental stretch all the time would lead to what the analytical gentlemen call 'listener fatigue.'

There must be variety: changes of mood, changes of angle, and of exposition. Going off at a tangent sometimes makes for variety in a straight talk, but this turning aside from the main theme has to be signposted all the way, and all the way back. The speaker knows when he is going to digress, and also knows when he intends to come back to the point of his talk—for it is all there in the script in front of him. But the listener doesn't know. He has been following the speaker along one line of thought, or narrative, or description, and suddenly the voice on the air changes course. The listener's immediate reaction is, "Now, where the blazes is he off to?" And by the time he realizes what is happening he has lost both the thread of the main theme and the beginning of the loose end that has broken away from it.

It is always worth saying that you are going to digress, and why. And when you return to the main part of the talk, it is also worth repeating the last point you made before you turned off, either by paraphrasing, or by saying the same thing in a different way.

In a well-composed talk, easy to listen to and helpful to later reflection, variety is achieved by making telling points at intervals. There is, in most talks, a certain amount of run-of-the-mill information which is relevant to your subject and has to be said: facts to buttress comment, background to throw something unusual into relief. How are you going to put this kind of information over? By leaving it as near the end as possible?

If you do this the second half of the talk will be like a solid pudding, and the listener—if he doesn't switch off —will think it is a pity that a talk which began so promisingly should turn out to be so dull after all. That will be his overall opinion of the entire talk—dull. It is an unfair opinion, because if a talk really were dull all through it would not get as far as the microphone; no producer would have accepted the original script.

The fact is, the listener is just as impatiently human in being irrational as the rest of us are. He does not stop to tell himself that the first part of the talk was good. The *impression* left with him is that of dullness. The speaker had not understood how to place his outstanding points, his highlights, at intervals throughout the talk.

'Placing' the highlights in a talk is a technique which should be studied, for it is the continual renewal of interest in a talk which keeps the listener's attention keyed up.

If possible the highlights should be connected with people. In the series by Julian Duguid, which I have already mentioned, there is a talk called "Mr Mascarenhas" which perfectly illustrates how effective it is to have a particular person as the apparent subject of a talk.

Mr Mascarenhas is introduced to us at the beginning, *in absentia*; he is late, like all Brazilians. When he does arrive, he is briefly described as a youngish, forceful man with a charming smile. That is the only explicit description ever given of him; but by the end of the talk we know a great deal about both Mr Mascarenhas and his fellow-countrymen.

We are aware of him all through the talk, though he actually says or does very little. He is there, in the background; the speaker brings him forward in the most natural way when it is necessary to underline a point about Brazilian customs or habits of thought.

The talk is not about Mr Mascarenhas. It is about Brazil; about coconut palms where the fruit hangs ripely and dangerously above the heads of the passers-by: about the new Brazilian nationalism and its possible repercussions on a factory in Yorkshire; about a remote, noisy town where cinema and church compete cheerfully over loud-speakers for custom: about the menacing silence in the low, hot scrub beyond.

By the end of the talk the listener knows what Brazil looks like and how modern Brazilians look at the world. He has even absorbed a few statistics, quite painlessly.

It is only after studying the talk later that one can realize how superbly planned it is; how skilfully Mr Mascarenhas has been used to focus the listener's attention every time the speaker wants to communicate solid, important information about a people and a country thousands of miles away. Just how important the speaker considers his subject to be—to the listener as well as to himself—comes out in his last few sentences.

Parker is a Yorkshireman who is finding it increasingly difficult to get his goods into Brazil:

> Parker was rather silent as he moved about São Afonso. It was obvious what he was thinking. Should he make his products in Yorkshire and trust to the market improving? Or should he take a jump and bank on Paulo Afonso and a new factory in Recife? He did not tell me his conclusions, and it was not my business to ask. Still, I should like to know: because that is the kind of question on which the future of England could turn.

I have discussed Mr Duguid's script at some length because it contains so much that—to me—makes a radio talk absorbing and exciting to listen to.

He has had extraordinarily interesting experiences, but he does not go on the assumption that a recital of his adventures is enough. He takes a *theme*, and builds it into a satisfying talk with a narrative of those experiences which will best fit the theme.

It is writers and speakers of such quality who can make the radio talk into an art.

8

STYLE AND CHOICE OF LANGUAGE

WE were listening to a novelist rehearsing a discourse, one which was full of smoothly rounded phrases and correct grammatical constructions. It was a good piece of prose—but it *was* a piece of *prose*, printed-word prose, not talk-prose. The producer sighed. It was going to take all his tact to induce the novelist to change that beautiful style so as to make it possible for broadcasting.

It is undoubtedly exasperating for a writer with a formed style to have to perpetrate several pages of script which *look* wrong. He has, at school, learnt the conventions of English grammar. At the university he has been given the great masters of literature as models for his style. Now, for broadcasting, he is asked to concentrate on clarity and vivid expression, and to let literary form go hang if need be. It takes much effort on his part to refrain from amending and tidying-up, and popping prepositions back in their proper places.

The experienced author, however, unless he is a dyed-in-the-wool purist, can generally change over to writing the spoken word without too much trouble. It is the occasional broadcaster who finds it difficult to express himself in the best way. He is not a writer in grain, but wants passionately to say something on the air. He does not know how to get it down on to paper, except in the form of an essay.

What is the right style for a radio script? Should you write exactly as you speak?

Heaven forbid. Listen to people talking: in buses, in restaurants, in shops. Listen to an acquaintance describing an experience to you. He will repeat himself, use the most hackneyed metaphors, interpolate irrelevancies, exaggerate. He will stop in the middle of a sentence, shrug, grimace, and expect you to know what he means. When at a loss for further description, he will say, "It was marvellous!" without giving any clue as to what he found to marvel at.

And if anyone could quietly take a tape-recording of you yourself talking in ordinary conversation the result would be equally enlightening.

'Natural' talk, for the purposes of a radio script, is an idiomatic and authentic expression of everyday speech, not an exact reproduction of it. Professor Vernon, in his inquiry, found that speech which was too conversational —with its frequent use of personal pronouns, repetitions, incomplete sentences, and implied familiarity with the listener—did not appear to make a talk easier to understand.

For my part, I think these tricks are more likely to hamper the listener in his attempt to follow a talk; they distract attention from what is being said to the person saying it—and sometimes give one an unpleasant impression that the speaker is trying to ingratiate himself with the listener.

The *rhythm* of ordinary conversation is a good guide for writing a talks script. If you actively listen to the way people talk you will find that you begin to be aware of a certain pattern of everyday speech. People do not talk —as they sometimes do in books—in very long sentences, with qualifying clauses. Neither do they talk in curt, complete sentences, after the manner of characters in a Noël Coward play. They talk in *phrases*, most of them short, some a little longer, but none really long.

A script built on this pattern, then, is likely to be easily understood, for it follows the listener's own usual speech-rhythm of short phrases, varied by occasional longer sentences. And they *should* be sentences. No carefully contrived, "Now then, let me see" interruptions, none of the "Ahs" and "Wells" and "Ums" which bespatter our usual flow of talk. Here is *selected* speech: everyday language which the listener is constantly hearing all around him, but which has suddenly become more sharply defined, catching and holding his attention, just because it is so familiar—and so different.

This brings us to the heart of the matter. The subject of your talk might be of urgent interest, but how are you going to get your listener to listen to it at all?

It is no use blinking the fact that the average talk does not command a very large audience. Talks on subjects of topical interest, especially if they are given by well-known people, send up the listening figures from time to time; but the general talk appeals only to a minority audience.

Some people listen to a talk because they have seen it announced and are interested in the subject. Others listen because they "quite like talks," and are curious to know what will come out of the lucky bag this time.

Then there are the hearers. These are the people who leave the radio-set switched on between two programmes which they actually want. Should your talk happen to be in the middle of this particular sandwich it is probable that you will be vaguely heard, not listened to.

This is a challenge. If your talk is interesting enough to turn a hearer into a listener you have accomplished something. You will not know whether you have done this or not; people do not often bother to write to tell you what a difference you have made to their cultural lives. But always remember the listener-on-the-fringe: the man who has listened to half the talk before he has realized he is listening at all—and who goes on listening because he finds it so absorbing.

If only a small minority of listeners to a talk listen because they are interested in the subject, it is obvious that a speaker's style and choice of words must be attractive enough to hold the casual listener. But, like many obvious principles in broadcasting, this elementary maxim is ignored in the most astonishing way by people ambitious to give talks. How do you think the following would sound on the air?

"The practicalities of personal advancement have never motivated A's procedures."

Sentences of that kind appear in scripts again and again. Jargon also comes into otherwise sound work. Here is a sentence written by a sociologist: ". . . Big hotels in all parts of the world are relatively undifferentiated." A radio producer would quickly change that to: "Big hotels in all parts of the world are pretty much alike."

Every time you use sentences that are difficult to follow, or words which the listener cannot at once understand, you are making his attention stumble. Professor Vernon found that up to half the population cannot give the meaning of words like "automatically," "equivalent," "expansion," "inevitable," or "analysis"; while only one in ten knows the meaning of words like "proximity," "function," "arbitrary," "impartial," or "remuneration."

It is wise to choose words which cannot be confused with other words that sound alike, but have a different

G   97

meaning. In most cases the context would be a guide to the listener, but there are some words—like "formerly" and "formally," for instance—which might pass for each other when said on the air, altering the sense of the passage.

"They had called formerly at the Residency."
"They had called formally at the Residency."

¶

I have tried, throughout this book, to stress the importance of simplicity: of the direct exposition of ideas, coherence of the narrative flow, and words which can be immediately understood. I believe these to be the fundamentals of good broadcast writing.

But now I am going to give, as an example of a magnificent radio talk, the work of a writer who followed no rules—for whoever heard of a genius following rules?

The late James Stephens had the gift of words. Beautiful, strange, fantastic words: his books are full of them. For broadcasting it was fantastic images which he conjured up, holding the listener in a spell, so that one didn't care what he was talking about—one only wanted the enchantment to go on as long as possible. Listen to this, from a talk called "An Irishman's Day," which he gave in 1945.

> *Some years ago I became very interested in words. I just adored a certain dictionary that said "Wine, weal, and winegar are werry good wittles, I wow," but I began to notice that there are certain things, quite a number of them, and we have no words to really describe them at all. 'Tis so with water. We have lots of dry words, for we are dry creatures, but at the best our wet words are only damp, and*

so we don't ever get intellectually or imaginatively at that element at all. . . .

One day, when I was right bothered about the fact that there are no wet words in the language, and that consequently one can't even talk about water, I decide to look into these matters for myself. So I took a header into the sea off a headland in Donegal. The water up there, that day, was astonishingly good-looking. It seemed to be made of sliding and surging rainbows, and the whole seascape had gathered together all the opals and rubies and emeralds, all the pearl-whites and jet-blacks of the world. So, right off that headland, in I plopped with a wriggle and a swish, and away I skimmed with a hum like the big bass string of a guitar.

Soon enough I was far out, and deep down, and wide away, and in less than no time I knew more about water than any chemist has ever dreamt of. . . . Thereon, soon enough and very shortly, I began to meet a lot of fish.

Well, the things I talked about to those fish would astonish you nearly as much as it astonished them. . . . Perhaps I ought to say at once that no fish I ever met with could understand the meaning of the word "wet" as applied to the element they lived in. "You're all wet," said I. One and all they asserted and asseverated, that they had never felt wet in their lives, and that water is whatever it is, but it is not wet.

He meets a lady fish, a very matron of fishes, as he travels about in the deep water.

She was about twenty-five feet long. She was three shadings of silver in colour—namely, pure silver, all shining; light-grey, all flickering; and pearly trimmings, all half hiding and coy. She was very elegantly, though massively, streamlined, and she had a ten-foot-wide tail, very delicate.

*very yielding, and stronger than steel. One swish of that
tail could drive her forward at about ten miles a minute. She
looked like lightning, and she moved like light!*

*I intimated to her that she was the darling of the world,
and she intimated back that she knew she was. She would
have been very vain but that she was very well bred; and a
certain careless vanity is very proper, very attracting, in
high breeding. . . .*

*We are now in deep water . . . we are bowered and
embowered in a translucent emerald, shot with golden spots
and laced with silver-sliding shadows. Here there is nothing
but the emerald, and the dull gold, and the silver, and if you
shut an eye there is the solitude, the almost nothing, the
almost nowhere, the all alone. . . .*

*A noise in water is a lot . . . louder than a noise in
air. And down there, in the grey-green, yellow-smelling
mid-deeps, when a periwinkle sneezes off the Irish coast
you can hear that sneeze bumping back off the Statue of
Liberty in New York Harbour. . . .*

It is difficult to get back to analysing talks after James
Stephens—who would have laughed aloud and chuckled
for minutes at the very idea of anything so prosaic as
taking a talk to pieces to see how it works. Yet—there
is the craftsman as well as the leprechaun of language in
Stephens. It is not by accident that he builds up his
climaxes, uses the unexpected adjective, the impish
image. His words on the radio are for speaking, every
time; he has you waiting for them—and gives you rich
value for your attention.

James Stephens's humour is on a plane of its own. His
passing left radio talks poorer in the realm of laughter,
as it did in the world of the imagination.

Humour has been called the lovable quality, and it is,

alas, a rare quality in radio. Sometimes there is a glint of it in a talk, but not often; allegedly amusing people are apt to sound forced when they try to be funny on the air.

Sarcasm—that sour sister of humour—is seldom effective in a talk. Irony, yes. But it needs to be used sparingly. The essence of ironic humour is lightness of touch, and astringency of comment must be matched by the tone and the manner of its saying. The slightest underlining, and it becomes either silly or clever-clever.

Wit is the most subtle form of humour, and much relished in a talk. Here, again, there is danger. On a platform, with the audience physically before him, the witty speaker can often get his point across without explicit statement. A look, a smile, a gesture—these may be enough.

On the air, where the speaker has to rely on words alone, the wit has to be put over with sureness, delicacy, and good timing. The listener here, whose criterion is Max Beerbohm, demands something approaching perfection.

Well, the script has been written, and is ready for the studio. Or—is it? The speaker reads it through, and wonders how much he should 'polish.'

This is a term used so often about written prose that it has become almost a convention that all manuscripts, like boots, should be well polished. The writing and rewriting are but the half of it, say the purists. What is really important is the final rubbing-up.

In the sense that a radio script can sometimes be made more logical and shapely, polishing may be a good thing. The remaining clichés could be thrown out, the trite phrase translated into a plain term. In theory—polish.

But I have found from my own experience that one

often polishes the spontaneity out of a talk. I have a liking for sparely written prose, and I am inclined to fine down sentences to their bare essentials when polishing or revising a script. Prolixity can be boring, but the other extreme often results in an effect of starkness and austerity which repels the listener.

If you have planned a talk well, and written it with enthusiasm, sensibility, and confidence in what you have to say, leave it at that.

9

REGIONAL AND OVERSEAS BROADCASTING

THERE are still people who think of regional broadcasting in terms of Mummerset, and all that it implies. These are, of course, metropolitans. People who live in the provinces know the value of the radio programmes which have been designed for their especial pleasure.

Regional broadcasts are sent out on wave-lengths which cover the territory in that particular part of the country; but they can be picked up in other places. They do not set out to replace the national programmes, any more than a good country newspaper sets out to replace the national Press. Regional programmes are of the greatest interest to the people who live in the regions, because they reflect a familiar way of living, and are often concerned with problems which have a down-to-earth application for local listeners.

There is a great deal of scope for first-rate broadcast talks in a region. The operative word there is 'first-rate.' The olde-worlde-quainte is no more wanted in a region than it is in London. The standard for both is exactly the same.

In a region the producer looks for two kinds of speakers. One is the specialist, the expert, the interesting personality who happens to live in that part of the country, and can give a talk on a subject not necessarily connected with the region. In other words, his talk would be just as suitable for the national services. But as he lives far from London, he is useful to know in his particular region; he can be called on for a talk when the occasion arises.

The other kind of speaker is more parochial, in the sense that his talk is of definite regional interest. There is a much wider range here than in the national services, where an enormously larger number of listeners has to be taken into account. A regional speaker can afford a more leisurely approach to many subjects of local interest, for there is a background, a basis, already established between him and his regional audience. In the West Region he does not need to explain at length where the Sound is: they know. In the North Region an industrial economy founded on wool and cotton, coal and steel, is taken for granted, together with habits of thought and a way of life natural to that part of the country. In Wales and Scotland, which run their own regions, there are plenty of opportunities for ding-dong talks and discussions on internal controversies.

A fair amount of interchange takes place between the national and the regional programmes. For instance, London regularly takes "Any Questions," which originated in the West Region, and is still their programme. The North Region's "Fifty-one Club" debates are also heard on the national wave-lengths. In the same way, good talks which have been heard in the regions are sometimes rebroadcast from London, even when they have a strong regional interest.

¶

There are two hurdles of which to be wary in regional broadcasting. The first is to be so filled with local patriotism as to be boring. A love of one's own corner of Britain is good to have, but it is not enough for a talk, unless the speaker has superlative powers of description, and an outstanding personality; or unless he has something striking to say.

The other hurdle is dialect.

Now, a dialect is not an inferior form of the main language, but a special form of expression within it. Dialect rises out of local needs. Regional industries have their own technical words and phrases which soon become incorporated in the local speech, and as town and countryside have differing needs and a variety of ways of living, dialect is charged with a richness of expression that gives it the vitality which standard English often lacks.

It can become debased too, and is often harsh and ugly. One of the problems a producer in the regions has to tackle is how far he should try to tone down a regional speaker's dialect in order that it should be understood by most listeners in the region. For there are many dialects within one area, and what is homespun to one set of listeners may be a bit of verbal fancy-work to another group.

One often meets with great sensitiveness over this question of using dialect in a radio talk. Sometimes it takes the form of inverted snobbery; I have heard a Lancashire speaker exaggerate his accent in the most truculent manner, for what was obviously this reason. His attitude was, "You think me common, don't you? All right, I'll show you."

I also once heard the mother of a young family declare that she would not allow her children to listen to radio programmes in dialect, as she wanted them to speak 'good' English. She did not remember that her children hear and speak dialect in the local schools. They hear a great deal of standard speech on the radio, and they accept the fact that there are two kinds of English: the language as spoken among themselves, and that spoken by their teachers and by announcers on the radio.

The sad thing is that, instead of being encouraged to recognize that a living language can contain both the homely form and a form which must necessarily be standardized to some extent, they acquire an inferiority complex about their own style of speech.

Continental people are much more realistic about this. Well-educated Dutch people speak in the local dialect at home as a matter of course, and in formal Dutch when the occasion calls for it. Swiss and German people rarely speak anything but their local patois informally among themselves, and High German in business and official life. If you listen to radio programmes on the Continent you will find that a substantial percentage of them are in the dialect of the station's particular region. So there is nothing 'common,' or inferior, about a talk in dialect.

Too much dialect, however, is tiring to listen to; and that is a good broadcasting reason why there should always be a sense of proportion when the question arises. Dialect gives flavour to a talk, provided it is genuine and un-self-conscious. When, however, it becomes self-consciously quaint, or incomprehensible, it becomes a bore.

¶

A study of *London Calling*, the overseas journal of the BBC, shows that there is substance in the remark made by a South American visitor to this country: "Britain has to export her best—and that includes talks."

The overseas services choose the best talks from the national and regional programmes to rebroadcast to the world, so unsolicited talks designed for these services have to reach a very high standard.

There are, broadly speaking, two kinds of talks broadcast in the overseas services.

One is the talk which projects Britain and the British way of life—our traditions, customs, politics, institutions, industries, and so on. Well-known people in their own fields are asked to talk about current affairs, the arts and sciences, national events. There are also programmes on the countryside, and on rural crafts and skills. Listeners in the Commonwealth, especially, have a great affection for talks on country matters.

The first thing you have to remember in planning this kind of talk is the very great difference between listeners at home and abroad. In the three services at home you have certain terms of reference. The Light Programme mostly caters for listeners who do not want anything too serious, the Third Programme is for listeners with academic tastes, and the Home Service comes somewhere between the two.

These are not watertight compartments; the same kind of people listen to both the Home and the Light, and occasionally to the Third. Still, you know fairly well who your listener is; you know you can both take a certain amount of common knowledge for granted. For instance, you do not have to explain who the leading politicians or comedians of the day are. You can talk about the weather without being thought crazy, and you can discuss sport idiomatically without anyone thinking you are describing a series of murders.

In the General Overseas Service, however, you are talking to a largely unknown audience, to people who do not know anything about Britain except what they read in their newspapers, hear on their own radio systems, or on short wave from the BBC. In the Colonies and the countries of the Commonwealth some listeners are likely to have visited the home country, and others will have read a good deal about it. But far more listeners will be ignorant of the majority of our habits and customs. Even in an English-speaking country like the U.S.A. there will be listeners with the most fantastic ideas of how we think and live over here. That has been well illustrated by Alistair Cooke in his talks on American life; he very often has to correct misconceptions which Americans have about us.

There are, too, many listeners in foreign countries who understand English, and who regularly tune in to programmes in the General Overseas Service. So it is important that not only must your ideas come through very clearly in an overseas talk, but your words and phrasing must be simple and absolutely without ambiguity.

This question of ambiguity is of the greatest importance, especially with an illogical language like English. You cannot, like Humpty Dumpty in *Alice*, make words mean just what you want them to mean: the foreign listener expects you to mean what the word *should* mean, according to what he learnt in his English lessons.

A subtle or literary style is, therefore, lost on him; it is more likely to puzzle and mislead than to impress him. Double negatives are particularly difficult for him to understand. "We, therefore, not unnaturally think . . ." might be worked out algebraically in his English textbook, but on the air it is better to say, "It is, therefore, not surprising that we think . . ."

If you have an idea for a talk accepted direct by the

General Overseas Service you can concentrate on the best style of writing to adopt for that particular audience, without having the home listener in mind too. But the technique of writing is quite different when you intend to submit a talk to one of the home services, hoping that it will also be accepted for the overseas service. The difficulty is to find a way of presenting facts which are likely to be known by the home listener, but which are unfamiliar to the overseas listener.

Not long ago I broadcast a talk in the Home Service which described a visit I made to three villages in Sussex. My aim was to give the listener some idea of the ancient ways of village life which still go on in an apparently sophisticated county near London, and how these old ways are being integrated into the rush of modern existence. It was a subject which I thought might appeal to the planners of the overseas services, so I tried to write it in such a way that, should they accept it for overseas, it could be recorded on transmission in the Home Service.

I wanted to give the overseas listener a picture of Sussex: the variations of downland and woodland, the deep-rooted customs and traditions. At the same time, I did not want to irritate the home listener with facts which he probably knew already. So I chose aspects of Sussex country life which were likely to be unfamiliar to the home listener, and more likely to be quite unknown to the listener abroad.

It would have been much easier to write two separate talks—and not half so interesting.

The other kind of talk for the overseas services is that aimed at a special country. Besides the General Overseas Service, there are programmes directed to nearly every country in the world. These are grouped into global regions; for instance, broadcasts to Canada and the U.S.A.

are given in the North American Service; those to Australia and New Zealand in the Pacific Service—and this also includes broadcasts to Fiji. There are separate transmissions to France, Scandinavia, and most other countries in Europe.

Many nationals from these countries come to Britain, either on visits or to live for a time. There are also British officials and business-men who have lived in foreign countries and are known there; they are likely to be listened to with interest.

I have met a great many visitors over here who have given charming and illuminating talks to their own countries; students recording their impressions of English university life, housewives relating how they try to acclimatize their families to our weather and our food, social workers describing their training. They come from India and Pakistan, from East and West Africa, from Cyprus and Jamaica and Newfoundland and Latin-America. I remember a girl from the Argentine who was studying visual aids in order to help with the literacy campaign in her own country; and an Indian girl film-director learning how to make documentary films. When they gave talks to their own countries they always related what they were doing over here, and what they hoped to do when they returned home.

The mere fact of being a foreigner in England does not automatically mean that you could do a good talk. But the visitor often sees our way of life through fresh eyes, and what he has to say might be of value to his hosts, as well as to his kinsfolk over the seas.

Part 3
SPEAKING THE TALK

10

VOICE AND MANNER

THE broadcaster of a talk has to do two things. The first is to write a text which has sufficient style and shape to be a decent piece of prose that will not sound 'prosy' when spoken. The second is to say this piece in such a way as to make the listener aware of a complete personality, not a disembodied voice. The speaker has somehow to translate the normal animation and gestures which a visual audience would see into certain effects in his voice.

These effects sometimes come quite naturally. A sensitive speaker will shade his voice and vary the tempo of his speech instinctively. If he has some dramatic power he will make his points with discreet emphasis, without any prompting from the producer.

But correct phrasing and variety of tone are technicalities. You can sit at a microphone chanting mi-mi-mi and practising inflexions and stressed syllables until your face muscles ache. The secret of communication is none of these things. What really matters is the *life* in your voice. This is something which no producer can put there for you. He may tell you that you sound flat or 'dead-pan' in the loudspeaker, and try to help you infuse some vivacity into your tone. But this is not a technical point, it is mainly a psychological one. You can only deal with it yourself.

The main trouble is probably the lack of response from others. When you are sitting talking to people in a room your style is bound to be tuned to the intimacy of friend talking to friend. You have the stimulus of answers to what you are saying—agreement or disagreement; but at least there is *some* response. Your voice accordingly charges itself with some emotion, quite automatically, according to the reaction of others.

At the microphone, though you may say exactly the same things, you have no one giving an immediate physical reaction. Instead, you find yourself reacting to your own state of mind. You imagine the audience—in millions. They are strangers. Instead of the sympathetic, or at least tolerant, attention of friends listening to you in the same room, their attitude towards you is, "Go on —interest me," and they cannot fill in your visual personality.

Because you know you are talking to strangers, you find it difficult to speak with normal feeling and expression. It is worse when you find yourself thinking of relations or acquaintances who might be listening with critical ears. Then your voice seems to sharpen itself without your volition.

This unfortunate reaction is more common than one might think. When I was editing one of my overseas programmes, a few years ago, I had to find a fresh speaker every week, and I came to understand the signs. If I heard a defensive or slightly aggressive note edging a speaker's voice, I would say, "You are thinking of someone in particular, aren't you?" And a typical reply would be, "Yes. My sister-in-law came along with me. She's in a listening-room. She thinks I'm going to make a fool of myself."

I have found from experience that one's mental attitude

has an immediate effect on the actual tone of voice during a broadcast. I am at ease when giving a talk only if I think of one person with whom I get on well. In my own case it is an old aunt in Devonshire. I know that she will be listening, and that she will be contented with what I have to say—whatever it is.

This has a quite extraordinary effect on my morale. I feel as if I am sitting with her, telling her about people I have met and places I have seen. The fact that she is affectionately interested does not make me careless, but the reverse. I want her to share the experience I am relating, and the only way I can do it is to speak as simply and clearly and naturally as possible.

This question of being natural is, of course, always coming up when radio talks are being discussed. The trouble is that at the microphone you cannot—unless you are exceptional—be natural. John Hilton, still held up as the greatest exponent of the art of sounding natural, used, in fact, to rehearse his apparently casual speech as carefully as an actor rehearses an important rôle. I found him a thought too casual, too 'natural.' I must admit, as a listener, to a liking for just that shade of formality in a speaker that brings with it a feeling of individuality.

Let me make it quite clear that I am not advocating formality in the usual sense. This too often turns into pedantry—the last thing one wants in a talk. What I have taken a strong dislike to is the excessive chumminess which some speakers develop at the microphone. I think it is an affront to the listener.

After all, one is not, in everyday life, immediately familiar with complete strangers. One treats them with some courtesy and a certain amount of that old-fashioned virtue, respect. I believe that even the present-day listener, conditioned to being called "mate" (or "dear," if female) by bus conductors, will feel his battered self-respect respond to the speaker on the radio who is pleasant and friendly, but who does not presume to greet him like an old pal.

Can one, then, sound friendly without sounding forced or phoney? Here, again, it is entirely a matter of mental attitude. If you truly *like* people—even though you find so many of them maddening, incomprehensible, or just plain awful—the chances are that you will be able to sound friendly and be quite genuine about it. If you are, by nature, repelled by people who are uncongenial, and inclined to armour yourself against life in general, you will find it difficult to infuse real friendliness into your voice.

This question of friendliness is a very tricky one, because, as we have seen, it is apt to sound forced. Yet it is one of the most powerful influences in broadcasting. What many of us sometimes forget is the enormous number of lonely people who respond to the friendliness in a radio voice. Psychologists would have a merry time with some of the people who write to broadcasters telling of their most intimate affairs, and saying what the voice coming out of the loud-speaker means to them. But loneliness is something one cannot argue about. It is all very well to suggest that lonely people should join clubs and societies. Many of them are not joiners by nature. They may be reserved, awkward in company, shy. But they are lonely, all the same, and the warmth and sympathy in a radio voice makes a great deal of difference to them.

¶

I think that quite a number of people with interesting things to say are inhibited from sending in scripts because they feel diffident about their accent.

This is a pity. If every broadcaster spoke standard English the result would be so monotonous that you would soon stop listening. The so-called Oxford accent, the Mayfair accent, the Kensington accent—they *are* all accents, and can be as difficult to follow at times as a Newcastle Geordie's plaited vowels. Standard English is without a regional accent, and therefore suitable for announcing, where objective presentation is required. It is not what to aim at in a talk.

English is a beautiful language—but what English? To my ear, most kinds of accented English, provided it is not slovenly or clipped. I remember a herdsman on a Welsh mountain, telling me about local rehearsals of the *Messiah*; his voice was without culture, but it lilted like a harp. I remember a Yorkshirewoman directing me to "Bootertoobs Pass." I can hear in my mind's ear a blunt Essex voice, and a rain-soft West Country voice, and the harsh flatness of a Midlands voice talking about bicycles. They each had individuality, a *tang*.

Speech is such a personal thing that it is foolish to try to change its chief characteristic, which is accent.

A producer will sometimes try to get a speaker to modify vowel sounds, but this will be for the sake of clarity, not for snobbish reasons. For instance, I recently heard a Cockney running over a talk with his producer. He was perky and amusing—but one couldn't understand half of what he was saying. The producer patiently set to work on some of his vowels—and the Cockney, who had an ear, co-operated wholeheartedly.

But apart from odd instances like this, a speaker who tries to change his natural mode of speech, hoping to sound like an announcer, will end by doing one of two things: if he is unsuccessful he will be caricaturing himself, and if he is successful he will have ironed away most of his individuality.

The most common way of trying to change one's accent is to attempt to make it more refined.

Refined speech is a bane. I once had a woman in my programme who had a personality with a punch, and a voice to match. During the preliminary audition and conversation she had been completely natural, but at the rehearsal before transmission she suddenly began to speak lake thees. She wuz soo tairibly refained thet Ai didn't knoo what Ai wuz gooing to do with har.

In the end I got her down to earth over a cup of tea in the studio, having first arranged with the programme engineer to begin recording while we were talking. It meant turning her talk into an interview, but there was no alternative. The programme was for an overseas service, and affected speech is anathema to listeners in the Dominions.

We are nearly all verbally lazy in conversation. We speak our native language idiomatically, but are constantly taking short cuts with words and phrases. The result is often slipshod, slovenly. It is here that an attempt should be made in improving one's speech.

This does not mean pronouncing every word with meticulous care, as foreigners do when they speak our language; you would sound pedantic. Nor does it mean a course in elocution. I should like to see a framed placard in the entrance hall of every radio organization:

ELOCUTION STRICTLY FORBIDDEN

If you listen to speakers on the air who do speak well you will notice that they give words full value, yet still sound unaffected and unacademic. Good radio speakers set a standard. In former days it was the theatre which was the model for speech. In every part of the country there were theatres where regular stock companies acted to crowded audiences. Their plays may have been compounded of blood and thunder, or lavender and sentiment, but their diction was admirable. And their audiences recognized that it was so, and appreciated it.

The theatre, except in London, has, in most towns, given place to the cinema; and one does not normally get a high standard of English diction in the cinema. It is now broadcasting which has an influence on people's speech, and a very powerful influence it is. That is why it is important that a slipshod manner of speaking should not be tolerated in a radio talk.

¶

Should one worry about the actual quality of one's voice for broadcasting? I know of one speaker who, after he had had his first script accepted, hired a tape-recorder so as to practise speaking. It took his producer a long time at rehearsal to get him to sound even normal, let alone natural.

Lecturers and actors use tape-recorders from time to time, but it needs a good deal of discipline and super-human objectivity to listen to your own voice and make a fair assessment of its quality. The usual reaction at first is outraged surprise; you cannot believe that you *really* sound so thin, or so syrupy.

The next stage is the dangerous one, when you think that perhaps you are not so bad as all that. Once admiration and self-satisfaction set in you start listening to the sound of your voice during the actual broadcast, instead of concentrating on what you are saying.

The real value of practising with a tape-recorder is to listen for mannerisms. It is these which disturb the listener's attention, and if you are ambitious to broadcast regularly it is important to be quite ruthless with yourself over any tricks of tone or speech which have crept into your voice.

An American writer states that the radio voice "must be healthy, well-dressed, and cheerful." That sounds very brisk and business-like. American radio studios seem to be full of breezy executives, smiling encouragement and assuring the broadcaster that he is certain to be O.K., butterflies in the stomach notwithstanding.

There is something in the American formula which could usefully brace up many of our speakers. If they could get even a fraction of American verve and buoyancy into the well-bred English voice it would make for livelier listening. But it is not easy to sound cheerful and buoyant when you are sitting alone in front of the microphone. Most producers I have met give one confidence, but the average British broadcaster is, as a rule, more diffident than his American counterpart.

To go back to mannerisms. The most noticeable one is a speech pattern. This can get on the listener's nerves as you go up-down, up-down, up-down. If you have ever sat through the Head's report at a school speech day you will know what I mean. The voice skis smoothly over the ground to be covered, and, instead of listening to the words said, you find yourself tracing the speech pattern—up-down, up-down.

There is very little time at rehearsal for the producer to attempt to change such a speech pattern in the speaker's voice. It is for the broadcaster to do it himself, well in advance. If your ear tells you honestly when you read aloud that you have a speech pattern—that is, a repeating pattern of any kind—remember that the operative word here is "read." The school Head is *reading* his report: that is why it sounds read.

If you think in terms of *saying* your script the pattern will be automatically broken by pauses which come naturally, and emphases which are inevitable.

Try to forget, too, any labels which friends and relations have attached to your voice. An admiring critic once called an actress's voice "velvety." After that there was no holding her, until a radio producer, rehearsing her for a broadcast play, said, "Don't sound so plushy, dear."

¶

Women's voices are more adversely criticized than men's voices on the air. One reviewer of my acquaintance, discussing this, said, "Women speakers either sound plummy and cosy, or schoolmarmy and 'county.'"

This had enough truth in it to sting. I thought of the occasions on which I should have liked to ask an outstanding woman to do a talk in one of my programmes, but did not, because the producer asked me to find a speaker with equal ability but a less crisp voice and manner.

It is inevitable, I suppose, that many women who have been in the rough and tumble of public life for a number of years should use the microphone as a megaphone. What a great pleasure and relief it is to meet the exceptions: those who can assert without sounding assertive.

I can think of about a dozen women's voices which are, to my ear, exactly right for talks broadcasting. Besides the individuality which each possesses, they all have certain qualities in common.

One is 'pleasantness.' This is an easy, friendly tone which cannot be assumed. It arises from that genuine interest in, and tolerance of, people in general—a quality already mentioned in a previous chapter as being one of the most important elements in broadcasting. It is at the opposite pole to the sweet, patronizing voices of some women speakers.

Another quality is that intangible thing, charm. Not the charm of the actress, which can often be turned on like a tap. This is the real thing, compounded of sincerity and kindness, and much else that one cannot easily analyse.

Perhaps the chief thing about my particular women speakers is their unbossiness. One is an Egyptologist of great erudition, another a Member of Parliament, a third a Royal lady, a fourth an eminent doctor, a fifth an announcer. They have quiet voices. They have dignity, but they do not stand on it. Listening to them, one is aware of humour, of a sense of proportion.

A critic who listens to scores of talks during the year says that he finds women's voices tiring to listen to, because most of them are so high-pitched. This is a natural phenomenon which the sex cannot help; most feminine voices have a higher register than those of men. (A woman speaker, listening recently to her unusually deep tones in a playback of a recording she had made, remarked, "My voice sounds as if it ought to have a moustache attached to it.")

It is said that the microphone itself is unkind to the timbre of women's voices, exaggerating deficiencies and sometimes causing a light tone to sound sharp or shrill.

Though, as I have said, women speakers are often

targets for strong criticism, it is, perhaps, some compensation to remember that the aforesaid critic added, "But when they do get to the mike they generally have something worth saying."

II

PRESENTATION: THE PRODUCER'S RESPONSIBILITY

A TALKS producer is a man (or woman) whose business it is to put a speaker on the air. He is responsible to the planners of the overall programmes for (1) finding the speaker in the first place, either by recommending an idea which has been sent in, or by inviting someone to give a talk on a selected subject, (2) auditioning the speaker, (3) obtaining a satisfactory script, (4) rehearsing the speaker, and (5) taking charge of the actual broadcast during transmission.

He also has administrative duties: preparing the publicity and announcement of programmes, booking studios, and so on.

A producer is trained to do a complicated and skilled job, and he is generally a person who has had wide and varied experience before coming into broadcasting. He also, as a rule, has far-reaching and diverse interests, and he knows where to go for information when he has no first-hand knowledge of a subject himself.

But he cannot be expected to know the background and techniques of all the talks which he has to put on the air; he is not a human encyclopædia, in spite of the astonishing amount of general knowledge which he acquires through meeting so many different kinds of people every week. If he is at all doubtful about the accuracy of any detail in a script it is his responsibility to check and cross-check against other sources of information at his disposal. Some speakers are liable to be offended at what they consider to be unnecessary fussiness, but it is essential if a high standard of accuracy is to be maintained.

If you have sent in a script that has possibilities it will be passed on to a producer to follow up. He will write to ask you to come along for an audition—a voice-test, to find out if your voice is suitable for broadcasting.

One of the most important qualifications a producer has to have for his job is an ability to get on with all kinds of people and to put them quickly at their ease. Producers become experts at recognizing the different forms that nervousness can take, and make allowances for it. A good producer can be a rock of confidence to the inexperienced speaker.

The audition is given in a talks studio. This is a small room, furnished with chairs, and a table, on which stands —or over which hangs—the microphone. Adjoining the studio, and separated from it by a large window, is the control cubicle. In here the engineer controls the technical side of broadcasting; it contains table-panels of dials and switches.

The producer settles you comfortably with your script in the studio, and goes himself into the control cubicle. You can see each other through the window, but cannot hear each other; you converse by microphone—there are loud-speakers in both rooms.

The studio in which you sit is completely insulated for sound; echoes and other extraneous noises have to be eliminated as far as possible, to ensure clear reception at the listening end. Because of this insulation you may have a slight shock when you first hear yourself speak in there, as your voice will seem to have lost all its tone. It won't sound like that to the producer; he will hear your normal voice in the loud-speaker.

He sits in the control cubicle, but he is not looking at you. He concentrates on listening. He may draw the curtains which hang on his side of the intervening window; it is easy to transfer the vivacity in a speaker's face to his voice, and the producer does not want to be distracted from the important job of judging your voice fairly.

He does not expect too much. What he listens for is a reasonably clear voice and some kind of definite personality. What he hopes for, of course, is someone with sufficient individuality to give the talk some distinction. But outstanding personalities do not turn up every day; and if the producer likes the script very much, and the voice is good, with personality coming through, even a little, he will make the best he can of the speaker's natural equipment.

You are not told at the audition if the talk has been accepted. If the producer is at all doubtful about your voice he will want to think about it before making a decision. There is nothing for you to do but to possess your soul in patience and wait to hear from him.

Once the producer is satisfied that your voice is suitable for broadcasting, he passes on the script to the head of his particular department, together with a note about the speaker's voice, qualifications for writing that particular talk, and anything else that is relevant. If this senior official agrees that it is a good talk and would interest listeners he passes the script on to the Controller of Talks, for final approval. The Controller is ultimately responsible for all talks that go into the programmes, and naturally must know what is being considered for acceptance.

The script has been passed, and is returned to the producer. He must now find a 'space' for it. A dozen other producers are also trying to find spaces for scripts which *they* have had approved. As there are comparatively few talks broadcast, compared with other programmes, the planners of the overall programmes have their work cut out, fitting appropriate talks into the available spaces— and satisfying all the producers who have talks waiting to be placed. That is one reason why, even when you have had a talk accepted, you may not be asked to broadcast it for many weeks.

Another reason may be that the talk is seasonable; for instance, a summer holiday talk is placed at the beginning of the summer, not at the end, and a talk on fashion during the period when the big London and Paris *couture* shows are on. Even if a talk is not tied to a particular season, it may have to give place to talks which are so tied. Again, the planners have to look at the entire picture of broadcasting over a three months' period at a time, so as to be able to offer as wide a variety of talks as possible. This may mean leaving certain subjects over to the next period.

¶

Having 'placed' your talk in the schedule, the producer writes to you, asking if the suggested date is a convenient one, and perhaps giving alternative dates. That item agreed, he asks you to decide on the final title for billing in the *Radio Times*, together with any information about the talk which can be compressed into two or three lines of description.

The talk has been accepted and publicized. Now it must be broadcast.

A rehearsal is fixed for the day before transmission. An hour—perhaps more—is asked for. It seems to you an unnecessarily long period in which to rehearse a short talk. You will come away wishing it had been longer.

You are taken to a studio—by now curiously familiar —and are given a copy of your script. The producer has a copy too. He asks you to run through the script, and this time he follows his own copy with a stop-watch and a pencil. His first job is to get the talk timed correctly, so that it fits into its allotted 'space.' Few people are able to write precisely the number of words which will fill the five, eight, or thirteen minutes which have been allowed for their talk. Experienced broadcasters over-write a little, as it is easier to cut out than to fill in at short notice. Inexperienced speakers invariably write too much, and are sometimes affronted at the very idea of cutting a line.

Why cannot they say it all, they want to know. They have gone to so much trouble to get so much in. Surely the next programme wouldn't mind starting a couple of minutes late?

The next programme *would* mind starting late. So would the next programme's listeners. And the people who habitually check their watches and clocks by the beginning of a programme would mind too.

I have listened to otherwise intelligent speakers arguing with producers on this point. The last word has to be with the producer, for he is responsible for getting the talk off the air, as well as on to it.

Once the script is timed, with a reasonable margin for further small cuts if necessary, the producer goes into the control cubicle and listens to the next run-through with a listener's ears. It is curious how words which looked right in the context of the script sound just wrong when spoken in the talk. No one can tell this until the talk is actually being rehearsed. You cannot judge for yourself when you are saying over the script at home, because you have thought of the words in the first place, and have got used to them—they sound all right by virtue of mere repetition.

But the producer, sitting by the loud-speaker in the control cubicle, is trained to notice what the listener will notice: a stiff phrase, an ambiguous word, an expression that bumps over a rut or two so that it seems stilted. A sentence suddenly comes out of the loud-speaker with a bang, a flourish. Slightly pompous? The speaker obviously does not mean it to be so, but it *sounds* pompous— and the producer makes a note on the script. The sentence will have to be rephrased.

Then there is the question of pronunciation. Many words can be pronounced in two or more ways, and when a question of this kind arises the producer refers it to a special department which deals with such queries. In general, they advise the version likely to be understood by the majority of listeners. But there are times when authorities clash.

I remember a programme when the pronunciation of the Dutch town-name Stavoren held up a rehearsal. The programme was a travel-talk with dramatized insets. An actress taking part in these pronounced Stavoren one way, the scriptwriter, who was also the narrator, pronounced it another way. She had been a on a visit to the town a few weeks earlier.

The actress, on first receiving the script, had consulted a Dutch friend on the pronunciation. The scriptwriter, having heard the inhabitants of the town pronounce its name, naturally thought that that was its general pronunciation.

She telephoned a Dutch official in London and asked for a ruling. The answer was that both pronunciations were used. She wrote a sentence into the script to this effect.

Here the producer was ready to hold up the rehearsal because of an unexpected snag. It was doubtful if any listener would have known or cared how Stavoren was pronounced, but it was worth spending time to get it right.

¶

Some speakers are naturals at sounding 'natural,' and the producer interferes as little as possible with their delivery. Most people, however, need expert advice in putting over their talk.

The producer has to use a good deal of judgment in helping different kinds of speakers. Those who tend to over-dramatize themselves must be tactfully steered into a quiet narrative style; others who sound flat in the loud-speaker are encouraged to let themselves go. Then there is the broadcaster who gives all the sentences in his script the same value, so nothing stands out, and there are no climaxes. The producer indicates where special points should be emphasized by a pause beforehand, and where to throw away lines, as an actor does.

A sensitive speaker quickly responds to these hints in technique, but some over-earnest speakers might be worried by them. The producer then has to decide whether his speaker is capable of picking up such points and profiting by them, or whether it is wiser to leave him alone and let the excellence of the material make up for any deficiency in presentation.

But, technical details of presentation apart, it is the producer's chief job to get his speaker to *speak*, and not to read. The listener knows quite well, if he stops to think about it at all, that the speaker has a script. But he is only really conscious of the fact if the speaker is obviously reading aloud.

It is a curious phenomenon of broadcasting that speakers who have written their own scripts, and therefore know better than anyone else what the sense of their talk should be, sometimes sound as if they were reading a page out of a book and did not know what was coming next.

A patient and skilful producer can make such a speaker re-think the original idea which is at the basis of the script, and encourage him to concentrate on the thought behind the words. If the speaker has the complete sense of what he is saying the producer does not bother overmuch with stresses and inflections; he knows they will come in the right places.

¶

Now comes the broadcast itself. You are asked to come some time before transmission. The script is ready for speaking; yesterday's alterations have been typed into a fresh copy for you.

If your talk has to be fitted into a magazine programme you will be asked to say your piece in the final runthrough of the entire programme. You may be asked to cut two or three more lines out of your script, to fit in with the overall timing of the full programme.

With a self-contained talk one run-through is sufficient if it has been thoroughly rehearsed on the previous day. There is time for the discussion of tiny details here and there—but no radical alteration is made, nothing that is likely to upset you or to make you feel more nervous than you probably are already feeling.

The producer shows you how to arrange the loose sheets of your script so that you can pick them up, one after the other, without rustling them. An engineer[1]—man or girl—has appeared in the control cubicle, and sits framed in the window. He asks you, through his microphone, to say a few words of the script, in order to adjust the level of your voice. He is quiet and relaxed; so is the producer—and so, you find, are you.

You are alone in the studio; the producer has gone out to join the engineer. He has told you that a red lamp on the wall will light up to indicate that your studio has become 'live,' and that he will flick a green bulb on the table as a signal for you to begin speaking.

There is a big, silent clock-face on the wall. It has a red second-hand, which you watch. For the first time you realize what the phrase "a split second" means. The hand moves round. The red lamp lights up. There is a flash of green on the table. You begin to speak.

You are on the air.

[1] Called a "studio manager."

12

PERSONALITY

PERSONALITY," wrote the schoolgirl, "is something everybody has got, only some people have got more of it."

I think that is as good a definition as I have come across; the dictionaries say the same thing in more learned language.

Most of us know what we mean when we say that someone has got personality, but we become vague and woolly when we try to pin down exactly what it is we do mean. *A* says it is a sense of strength coming over from someone with a plus-one character; *B* says it is someone who knows his own mind; *C* says it is the projection of confidence which comes from knowledge; *D* says it is a feeling of abundant and overflowing life; and *E* says it is charm—that dangerous quality.

It is all these things, and a good deal more. For me, it also includes zest. Not heartiness, or chumminess, or any brand of synthetic good-fellowship which has implicit in it patronizing overtones. Zest is essentially subjective. A speaker who can convey his own enjoyment in what he is talking about without having to *tell* the listener how enjoyable the enjoyment is has got zest in its purest essence. Zest often has a rousing pagan strand in it—an unashamed capacity for getting the best out of life. Robust characters, those who seem to have an extra-large-size dynamo packed into their skins, have zest for their motive power.

But it comes through in quiet voices even more strongly than in forcible ones. It is unmistakable, for instance, in Alistair Cooke's distinctive, humorous tone as he describes the American scene in his weekly broadcasts. He never tells you that he finds this or that incident earth-shaking or soul-searing. He simply tells you about the incident. But, whatever he has been doing or seeing or hearing, he somehow communicates his own zest for living, together with the hard-core facts about snow in New York or the wart on a Senator's chin.

I should put warmth and sympathy as important qualities which make the speaker intensely individual to the listener. Energetic heartiness has often been tried as a substitute for vigour, and soft soap for warmth and sympathy, but the bogus 'personality' speaker soon shows up on radio. One cannot say anything about these two precious qualities, warmth and sympathy, beyond the fact that some people are born with them, and others are not, and the microphone seems to be curiously sensitive in projecting these elements in a speaker.

¶

Individuality is perhaps the most important thing in broadcasting. On the entertainment side—in variety and drama—it is the one thing that matters above everything else. A player or comedian with a showman's personality can amuse, impress, infuriate, or enchant the listener even when his material is poor; whereas one with a colourless personality could not put the best written script over on the air.

But actors and comedians in the entertainment industry have been *chosen* mainly for their personality, and programmes are specially written to exploit their various talents. The listener switches on to hear Josh So-and-so in the Turn-it-on-here Show, or the team of Fiddle-faddlers in their weekly half-hour spot. They know that Josh is always a scream, and that the F-Fs made them laugh last week and will probably put over some funny cracks this week.

There have been a few talks broadcasters with 'personality' reputations. The late John Hilton was one; he could be sure of a large number of listeners, whatever he was talking about. And there were hundreds of people without gardens who used to listen to Mr Middleton, on Sunday after Sunday, just to enjoy his slow "Good afternoon," and deliberate manner of talking.

There are still some speakers with a special quality of voice or delivery which fascinates the listener; you keep the set switched on even when you do not understand much of what the speaker is saying. Many listened to Fred Hoyle talking on astronomical physics, and to Bertrand Russell talking on philosophy, without being able to grasp the meaning of a quarter of what was being said. In each case the personality of the speaker—based on the authority of a first-class intellect—was sufficient to keep the ordinary listener absorbed.

The majority of talks broadcasters, however, are listened to for information. The speakers are expected to be intelligible and sufficiently pleasant to listen to. Outstanding individuality is not demanded—though there is a quick response to a speaker when he does turn out to have that 'something' which makes him different from everybody else. It is the potential speaker with the plus-something for whom the producer is always looking.

For this reason, beginners in radio who are ambitious to work regularly in the medium sometimes try to model themselves on personality broadcasters. What they too often succeed in doing is to collect a row of microphone tricks—mannerisms, telling pauses, unexpected chuckles ("Doesn't he laugh naturally—just like a real person!")

But to copy a popular radio personality is to handicap yourself from the start. You cannot become a carbon impression of another person. You cannot simulate some one else's highly individual quirks of character. The fact of trying to copy another person automatically puts you into the bogus class of speaker, for imitation is not flattery in this case—it is an admission that you have no individuality of your own, and must borrow another's reflection.

Can a radio personality be deliberately cultivated? I think it can.

What you must do, I believe, is to find out if you have qualities which can be developed for radio speaking. This is a question for you yourself, and not for psychologists, relations, friends, and pep-talkers. The main thing is not to bamboozle yourself, not to fit yourself out mentally with qualities and characteristics which you know you do not really possess.

It may also mean trying to loosen inhibitions in sides of your nature which you know exist—gaiety, quick sympathy, light-heartedness. We are still, as a nation, very Puritan in many ways; we tend to shove much of our natural warmth and friendliness into moral straitjackets. It is not easy for us to 'loosen up' until we know people very well. It is this reserve, this stiffness, which gets in the way of good broadcasting. The speaker who can break out of it, so that the listener is aware of the essential person behind the voice, brings himself as well as his script to the microphone.

There is always a risk, of course, in trying to 'develop' personality. True personality is an unconscious thing, and when you begin to exploit foibles you may do it at the expense of your integrity.

'Integrity' is a word which has become very fashionable in broadcasting. If a speaker is rude or brash, saying things for effect, attacking institutions or national characteristics with cheap gibes—he is said to have 'integrity.' The real meaning of the word is probity, and it has nothing to do with this new, so-called frankness.

The core of personality, it seems to me, is integrity in its true sense; bringing out and making the best of what is actually there. You may find that the personality which emerges does not have a popular appeal. But at least it will be the real thing.